EDOUARD RODITI

EMPEROR
OF
MIDNIGHT

Black Sparrow Press • Los Angeles • 1974

LIBRARY OF CONGRESS CATALOGING IN PUBLICATION DATA

Roditi, Edouard.
    Emperor of midnight.

    I. Title.
PS3535.0338E4   811'.5'2   74-17017
ISBN 0-87685-186-3
ISBN 0-87685-185-5 (pbk.)

The etching on the cover is by Jose Hernandez

Many of the poems and prose-texts included in the present volume
have been previously published, often in an earlier version which
has now been revised and edited for publication here. The periodicals
from which such previously published texts have been collected in-
clude the following: *Blues, Cahiers de l'Etoile, Deliria, Horizon, Kayak,
New Directions Annual, Pagany, Sir Galahad, Sumac, Tambour, The
Adelphi, The Cherwell, The Oxford Outlook, transition, Tree, VVV.*

TABLE OF CONTENTS

Preface 7

Emperor of Midnight [1927-1932]

Oracles 17
The Prophet Delivered 25
Letters to a Murderer 34
Prayers at Dawn 37
Sea Lost Soul 38
Arrival in the City of Dreadful Night 39
Poem 40
Solar Myth 41
Poem 42
For Alice Nikitina 43
Avatar 45

Prose Prose [1929-1932]

The New Reality 49
Preface to an Autobiography 53

Prose Poems [1929-1973]

The Rise and Fall of the Roman Republic 59
Through the Needle's Eye 66
Psychological Novelette 77
Letters from a Lost Latin Empire 81
Selective Service 85
Question Period 86
The Conspiracy 87
Dialogues and Monologues Overheard in the
   Fire that Refines 92

New Hieroglyphic Tales [*1929-1968*]

Foreword to the 1968 Kayak Press Edition 97
Myths & Marvels 99
Mirages 109
Description of the Last Woman 112
The Pathos of History 115
Journal of a Trip 118

Inventions [*1938-1970*]

The Fall of Man 127
Poem about Nothing 129
The Customer is Always Right 130
Four Allegories of Love 131
Manhattan Novelettes 134
The Identity of Contraries 136
The Nature of Knowledge 137
Cold War Bulletins 139
North Beach, San Francisco 141
Catoptomantic Poem 142
The Egocentric 143
Obituary for a Bedbug 144
Household Hints: A Bestiary 145
The Secret Ship 146

PREFACE

Even if they appear here for the first time in print, some of the Surrealist texts included in the present volume were written as early as 1927, though they have all been revised more recently, to avoid unnecessary repetitions. Other texts, likewise revised, are reprinted here from periodicals that have become rare and are now accessible only in a few specialized libraries, or else from my earlier volume of *Poems 1928-1948*, published in 1949 by New Directions and long out of print. To these, I have added all of my *Prose Poems: New Hieroglyphic Tales*, first published by George Hitchcock as one of his Kayak Press books and now out of print, as well as a few recent prose-poems that may well illustrate a more consciously ironical or satirical phase in the evolution of a Surrealism which remains intrinsically subversive in its rejection of reality and its determination to transform it, whether in terms of the sublime or of the absurd. Individual poems and prose texts have been dated here, whenever possible. But the collective publication of such a diversity of poems and prose-texts, written at various times between 1927 and 1973, may well require some explanatory comments.

Especially in recent years, readers of some of these texts have suspected me of having originally written them under the influence of some hallucinogenic drug. Without being at all puritanical, I have never felt, for reasons of my own, the desire or the need to become habitually addicted to any of the various "aids" of the kind which so many of my friends have used and then recommended to me. Throughout the years of my adolescence, I had been frequently exposed to neuro-psychiatric experiences, known as "anterior temporal lobe seizures," which had the one felicitous effect of dispensing me from ever needing to have recourse to drugs in order to obtain access to those "other" states of being or "other" worlds which many of my contemporaries are so anxious to explore. At one time, I was thus being treated in Paris by the same neurologist as Antonin Artaud, for these seizures as well as for asthma and other mysterious "allergies to reality" which repeatedly condemned me for long periods of time to a somewhat lonely and withdrawn life.

Though born of an American father, I was then living in Europe and had become acutely conscious of being an alien

7

wherever I went, in spite of my fluency in at least three languages. In my solitude, I kept busy, however, by reading a great deal of poetry of the past, in English, French, Latin or Greek, sometimes also in Spanish. After 1930, I began reading German and Italian poetry too.

I was sixteen when I first chanced to meet in Paris the Surrealist poet Georgette Camille. Through her, I soon began to associate also with her friends Robert Desnos and René Crevel, later too with a group of younger "dissident" Surrealist writers, among others Roger Gilbert-Lecomte and René Daumal, who were then publishing a periodical entitled *Le Grand Jeu*. Before associating with any of these French Surrealists, I had already been reading William Blake, especially some of his "prophetic" writings, and had even chanced to read all of Edward Young's *Night Thoughts*. Now I began to read Rimbaud, Lautréamont, Nerval and the French Surrealists too. A year later, in 1927, I was trying my hand at what we believed to be "automatic writing."

My first experiments in this field produced only garbled but recognizable echoes of my extensive and varied readings. I had memorized too much and had not yet found access to the source of any truly personal vision or poetic idiom. But Robert Desnos encouraged me to continue, perhaps because I shared with him a remarkable facility to withdraw from my surroundings and, even in the midst of a noisy crowd of friends, to write feverishly and as if in a trance, without hesitation and without stopping to find the right image or the right word. His own mind was so saturated with his readings of Rimbaud that some of his automatic writings led André Breton and other Surrealists to believe, for a while, that Rimbaud's spirit might well be dictating his lost poems to Desnos, who would be simply transcribing them in a trance similar to that of a medium in a spiritualist séance.

During one of my periods of illness when I had to spend three months in a Swiss nursing-home, I translated Saint-John Perse's *Anabase* into English, without knowing that T. S. Eliot, with the author's permission, was already engaged on the same task. Since I could not obtain the French poet's permission to publish my own translation, I sent a copy of it to Eliot, who invited me to come and discuss with him our different interpretations of particularly difficult passages of *Anabase*. In the final version of his translation, Eliot even adopted a few of my interpretations and suggestions; but he was also kind enough to express interest in seeing some of my own poems.

If I remember right, I first showed Eliot a series of relatively early poems, *Oracles*, which he read and returned to me a few weeks later with his extensive annotations and suggested corrections. In spite of this encouragement, I no longer considered the corrected version of *Oracles*, when I was eighteen, worthy of publication. I had reached the point, some months earlier, where my more recent "automatic writing" no longer echoed as recognizably the style or the contents of my readings. My poetry had in fact become a way of feeling and of living rather than of mere writing.

I was already publishing some of these new English or French poems in *transition*, *Pagany*, *Blues*, *Tambour*, *front* and a few French periodicals too. When I appeared as an undergraduate student at Oxford University, I thus attracted some attention because I had just published "The Prophet Delivered" in *transition*, to which Joyce and Gertrude Stein were regular contributors. Together with a couple of other Oxford undergraduates, I then attempted prematurely to start an English-speaking Surrealist movement and, a few months later when I was nineteen, *The Oxford Outlook* thus published in 1929 my hurriedly written manifesto, "The New Reality," which I now reprint here.

The English poet Bernard Spencer was the only other member of our little group who continued, as I did too, to write and publish after I left Oxford that same year and we parted. All the other undergraduate Oxford poets of our generation, Stephen Spender, Louis MacNeice, Richard Goodman and Clere Parsons, were more or less under the influence of W.H. Auden, who had left Oxford a year earlier. They thus refrained from joining our Surrealist group, though Clere Parsons, who was an admirer of E.E. Cummings and of Gertrude Stein, was distinctly sympathetic to our aspirations.

Our manifesto went almost unnoticed in Oxford, but aroused some interest among some Cambridge undergraduates, especially Hugh Sykes-Davies and Malcolm Grigg, who were then publishing *Experiment*. Some years later, by a mysterious kind of literary osmosis, my manifesto also began to bear fruit in the early writings of poets who had probably never read it: George Barker, David Gascoyne, Charles Madge and Dylan Thomas, among others.

Around 1930, only my more apocalyptic Surrealist poems were being readily accepted for publication in the few little magazines, mainly "expatriate," to which I had access. Even the editors of *transition* seemed to prefer them to my experiments in realms of the Surrealist absurd. Nor is this surprising. Most historians of Surrealism, such as Maurice Nadeau in France and Anna Balakian in America, still attach more importance to the romantic quest of the absolute or the sublime, as revealed in most of the poetry of Breton, Eluard and René Char, than to the "black humor" and the anarchist cult of the absurd that are both so admirably exemplified in the writings of Benjamin Péret.

French literary Surrealism indeed owed its birth to a strange marriage of Heaven and Hell, or rather of the sublime and the absurd, that William Blake might well have imagined; in fact, in terms of literary history, to an unexpected alliance of romantic mysticism, inherited from Novalis, Nerval, Baudelaire, Rimbaud or Mallarmé, and of post-romantic or realist spoofing of the kind that, from Flaubert's *Bouvard et Pécuchet* and the farces of Eugène Labiche, leads to the absurdities of Alphonse Allais, to the truculent black humor of Jarry's *Ubu Roi* and to Dada nihilism. But the Surrealist cult of the absurd proved for a long while to disconcert even more than its quest of the sublime. Only in recent years have Surrealist "black humor" and experiments in the absurd been granted more serious attention.

In the early Thirties, English-speaking Surrealists, whether in England or in America, found scant encouragement. After the 1929 Wall Street Crash, even the few "expatriate" American magazines that had begun to publish Charles Henri Ford, Parker Tyler, Paul Frederic Bowles and me, the four youngest contributors to *transition*, soon disappeared. I then found myself encouraged only by Eliot in London and, in distant Chicago, by Harriet Monroe, the distinguished founder and editor of *Poetry: A Magazine of Verse*. Both of them, however, encouraged me only to write and publish an entirely different kind of poetry. If only for my own pleasure, I continued nonetheless to write some Surrealist texts, whether in poetry or in prose, though I no longer found occasion to publish them.

In my own mind, I could distinguish quite clearly the two kinds of poetry that I was now writing. In 1949, when I published in New York, with New Directions, my volume of collected *Poems: 1928-1948*, I therefore called "inventions" the few Surrealist poems that I included, but all the other poems "imitations." Paul Goodman was one of the very few American poets and critics who understood immediately that I thereby intended to distinguish poetry which remains in the Humanist tradition of imitation of the ancients and of Platonic emulation of existing models from a more Romantic or post-Kantian conception of poetry as pure self-expression and as invention of unique experiences in themselves.

Only in 1968 was I at long last offered by George Hitchcock an opportunity to publish, with Kayak Press of San Francisco, a volume of my Surrealist prose-poems, a few of which had already appeared in periodicals as early as 1928. Most of them, however, had never yet been printed. From 1935 until quite recently, I found myself able to publish so few of my Surrealist writings in England or in America that I had almost given up all hope of ever publishing them, although Allen Ginsberg and Gregory Corso repeatedly told me that they certainly should be published.

To English and American readers, Surrealism should never have seemed as alien as some hostile critics have claimed. Even the French Surrealists, in spite of André Breton's preposterous ignorance of everything that had not been originally written in French or that failed to attract his attention in a French translation which, all too often, was mediocre or unreliable, were well aware of the fact that English and American literature had never been as dominated by rationalized thought as the literature of France. In his Surrealist halcyon days, Louis Aragon thus translated, with the encouragement and help of Nancy Cunard, Lewis Carroll's *The Hunting of the Snark*, and Antonin Artaud translated *The Monk*, the great "gothic" novel of Matthew Lewis, and also Shelley's verse-drama *The Cenci*, which he adapted and produced on a Paris stage. In a number of French Surrealist texts, one also finds Edgar Allan Poe, William Beckford, Thomas De Quincey and William Blake variously mentioned or praised as literary ancestors of the Surrealist movement. To these names I would readily add those of Horace Walpole, author of another great "gothic" novel, *The Castle of Otranto*, and the first, in his little-known *Hieroglyphic Tales*, ever to have experimented, in the Surrealist sense, in automatic writing; of Robert Maturin, author of *Melmoth the Wanderer*, another fine "gothic" novel; of Charles Brockden Brown, the American whose "gothic" novels, *Alcuin* and *Wieland*, contain passages of truly visionary grandeur; of James Thompson, the laudanum-addict and visionary poet of *The City of Dreadful Night*; of Ambrose Bierce, whose tales of *The Parenticides' Club*, especially "Oil of Dog," can easily vie, for sheer truculent absurdity, with *Ubu Roi* and anything else that Alfred Jarry wrote in French; of Artemus Ward and Petroleum V. Nasby, whose journalistic extravaganzas often reveal a rare but typically American gift for the absurd, and of Joseph Smith, the Mormon Prophet, to whom *The Book of Mormon* was dictated, in a

11

naïvely Biblical style worthy of some literary Douanier Rousseau or Facteur Cheval, by a supernatural being while he himself was in a trance.

In my own development as a Surrealist writer, I have always been keenly aware of possible affinities with these many English or American antecedents. Though it has not always been easy for me to free myself, in automatic writing, from the guiding hand of reason, I have avoided recourse to the use of drugs: my frequent experience of the hallucinatory phenomena of the epileptic aura provided me for many years with a sufficiently easy access to alienation from day-to-day reality and to an awareness of the existence of "other" areas of experience. Anyone who is fairly frequently visited by experiences of *déjà vu* or of alienation from reality no longer "finds" hallucinogens "necessary," and I was even able to train myself, after a while, to experience these phenomena or to avoid them almost at will. In "The Prophet Delivered," I was yielding to the kind of trancelike experience of being "possessed" that Blake and Joseph Smith had both known: the poem was then "dictated" to me, as if my a mysterious extraneous power that had risen from within myself or that descended upon me from elsewhere. In "How Rome Was Built in a Day," on the other hand, I allowed free associations to lead me, in automatic writing, into the same kind of world of absurd fantasy as Horace Walpole reveals to his readers in his *Hieroglyphic Tales* or as Raymond Roussel describes in his *Impressions d'Afrique*. But the narrative which I have finally decided to publish here is a much later revision of the text which I had originally written as only one episode of a whole series of such narratives. I intended to publish them all as *The Rise and Fall of the Roman Republic*; unfortunately, I have somehow mislaid, since 1929, most of this manuscript, so that the sample chapter published here has had to be reconstructed from fragments and from memory, though without allowing rational criteria of verisimilitude to interfere in the dreamlike absurdity of the events described.

Between these extremes of the apocalyptic sublime and of absurd fantasy, my other Surrealist "inventions," first collected here or reprinted from the *Prose Poems* that I published in 1968 with Kayak Press, cover a fairly wide range of remembered dreams, or verbal daydreams, of allegory, of fable and of the kind of satire that still owes some of its derisive nihilism to Dada. Sometimes, the writing of a remembered dream has led me into a new daydream that expanded it or added new dimensions of meaning. Surrealism indeed stresses the importance of freedom and, in spite of André Breton's paradoxical authoritarianism as its almost papal founder and leader, should never be too rigorously orthodox.

In the present volume, I have collected some later prose texts which George Hitchcock excluded from my *Prose Poems* because he felt that they were more narrative than lyrical, such as the "Psychological Novelette," first published in New York during the War in *V.V.V.*, and "Through the Needle's Eye," which is now published here for the first time.

"The Prophet Delivered" is published here in full for the first time. Its first canto had originally been published in 1928 in *transition*, its second canto a few months later in *Galahad*, an Oxford undergraduate publication where one can also find early poems of Spender and MacNeice. To these I have added, in addition to the Surrealist manifesto, "The New Reality," a number of other poems, including the revised version of *Oracles*, which were all written between 1927 and 1930 and some of which were then published in various English, French, American or "expatriate" periodicals, as well as the unpublished "How Rome Was Built in a Day."

Between 1930 and 1940, I could find no editors willing to publish any of my Surrealist texts, and many of those that I then wrote seem to have been lost in the course of my many removals. Only *The Adelphi*, in London, dared publish a few sample pages from "The Apprentice Cabbalist," included here. Some day, I may find in an old file a few more sections of this short book, the rest of which was never published. *The Adelphi* and its editor, Sir Richard Rees, were in those years very eclectic and daring: they were already publishing Dylan Thomas and George Orwell too.

Finally, I have included here a few more obviously Surrealist lyrics which had already been published by New Directions in my *Poems 1928-1948*, now out of print, and a few recent prose-poems. In these later pieces, I accept reality as if it were a found object of an ambiguous nature that can lend itself to several interpretations. Those that I choose remain, of course, the ones which reveal most clearly my sense of being personally threatened by reality as an alien and hostile force. In a way, I have never been an autistic Surrealist of the kind that, like the "divine" Marquis, tends to the contrary to threaten reality and the outside world.

Edouard Roditi
Paris, 1974

Emperor of Midnight
(1927-1932)

ORACLES

*"Entre le vide et l'évènement
pur . . ."*   Paul Valéry

I.

My will cannot yet force
The fateful buds of speech,
Nor can I speak my thoughts:
My lips are sealed with sleep.

"Silence is law," the stars complain,
Sworn to eternal secrecy,
And how can I repeal such stern
Decrees of doom, redeem the stars?

The sky oppresses me, its vault
Of stone-grey clouds has kept my mind
Imprisoned in sepulchral gloom
Where subterranean streams of dream

Flow endlessly. A seal is set
On my numb lips and stricken mouth
While foul and acrid fumes beget
Dim visions in the white-hot glow

Of my drugged eyes. My hands are weak
And the walls of my prison of prophecy
Bruise them and contain my cries
That only I can hear. Were I

Now free I might announce to all
A realm of bliss, with festooned trees
Shading our blessed heads beneath
Their fronds while the sun's lion-rampant

Grows frenzied in its fires of gold.
But jealous gods govern the flow
Of my utterances, censoring
All promises of future peace.

17

Could but the cleansing ocean
Wash from this dark earth its stains
When the setting sun pours its purple wine
Into the sleepily stirring waves

And the traced coasts form a mixing-bowl,
Then might I venture to foretell
The golden age for which I pray,
When misery must flee these shores

Like flocks of birds that with harsh cries
Avoid the winter's colder skies,
While joy would crystallize like frost
On the day's clear pane, and never melt.

II.

Rain casts and drags its net
Across the street. The night
Is caught in mists, the stars
Are caught in mists, my lips
Are caught, with all the stars.

My lips are frozen and
The night lasts all too long,
Breathing a spell of death
On its halted flow of hours.

Like icicles, my speech
Hangs in the night, the words
That I might speak have died,
Still-born the words that I

Would speak. The rain breaks paths
Of silence through the night
That with its bitter breath
Has sealed my lips. The stars

Are dimmed by mists. The words
That I might speak are ghosts.

III.

Faint shadows haunt me
With unuttered warnings
Of the lipless dead whose speech
Is too shrill for human ears.

The trees are tripods for the seers
Whose words must justify the night.
Their shaftlike trunks are blurred
By mists that slowly rise

Till I perceive, seated aloft,
My sibylline companions
Whose songs, like rustling leaves,
Foretell the past, remember the future,

In a timeless trance. Were I as wise
As these birdlike seers, well might my spells
Begin to emulate their songs
As they croon and twitter in their nests,

Swayed by the wind. Gently breathing
Through the thick foliage that conceals
Them in its bowers, the evening breeze
Draws music from the quivering leaves . . .

In the arcades of the grass
The glow-worm glistens and, at night,
Great cities revel in the turmoil
Of avenues bright with false daylight

Where solemn statues watch,
Tired of their stony fate
That robs their lips of speech.
A maze of roads still leads

To countless Romes and Troys
Where crowded streets provide
A pageant of mortality:
Merchants whose beards conceal

The twitching of their nervous lips
As they calculate their risks, or priests
Who have lost their faith and pray
Like actors, false prophets quartering

The future like a carcase sold
Piecemeal, warriors too who seek
To drown in drink the memory
Of bloodshed, all afraid of death

But grateful for the life they waste
So lavishly while they go their ways
And busily display their folly
As mummers in their dance of death.

IV.

The soil exhales its mists around
The surging oaks whose tense trunks prove
The earth is male, its paramour
The weak and yielding air where birds

Chatter their news of love and food.
My riddles are unsolved. The night
Invades my mind again, its dark
Waters flooding the plains of thought.

My dreams, I know, might not come true
For countless teeming years that lie
Still sleeping in time's womb. My head
Is meanwhile loud with alien visions.

I seem to watch them from afar
Pitching their tents, a nomad horde
From nowhere come to camp awhile
In the fertile fields of illusion.

Can other men distill
The honey of their clouded thoughts
More clear? True, I have known
Men whose words flew heavy-burdened

With thick pollen of meaning; nor are
My words like theirs. And others
Whose words buzzed like disordered swarms
Of noisome flies; nor are

My words like theirs. Clouds pass
And cast their shadow on my brow,
Confusing my thoughts. My lips
Utter these words that in my ears

Complain and then, set down upon
This page, complain before my eyes.
Even to me, who speak and write,
They're meaningless, a senseless sound.

Constricted here and now, they seek
To tell of time and place that are
Both infinite. Fettered by dreams
I'm doomed to fail whenever I speak.

V.

I wade in dreams and feel
How soft they cling. My feet
Tread hidden floors and paths of cloud.
I may not know where these paths lead

My dreaming feet that tread
An endless maze of shifting clouds.
I cannot see my stumbling feet
That wade in dreams. I walk as if

Asleep or treading soil that yields
Beneath my hidden feet. Like cloaks
That wrap my feet, these clouds conceal
My path, their soft embrace

Like that of quicksands. Who has set
For me these snares whose clammy hold
Upon my feet I cannot break
As I wander in my dream of death?

VI.

My star has pierced the gloom that cast
Its crippling spell upon my speech
And, shining, leads me now to choose
At last the words that fit my thoughts.

But to my star's message of hope
The constellated towns respond
With lights that like a captive's eyes
Greet sadly this belated freedom.

My hand contrives to spell the words
That, runelike, should be carved in rocks
And then desists, for all my dreams
Must fail to warn you of your fate.

Who are these men whose feet
Have traced their tracks upon my path,
Embroidered with their footprints, proof
Of many generations in this land,

Of countless feet that have come by
My resting-place and of more men
Now dead than all who still breathe air?
Oh land whose paths are smooth as pebbles,

Whose fields bear scars of countless ploughs,
Why do you not yield your hidden history
In the cryptic latin of inscriptions?
Why refuse to reveal at once

Your hoarded treasures, buried temples,
Kitchen middens, devastated cities,
Forgotten cemeteries, broken potsherds,
Stones carved with words that bring us news

Of other ages, a palimpsest
Of deeds and thoughts of men whose names
Are lost for lack of chronicles
To record for us their wasted lives?

The sea's the symbol of a truth
Immutable, for all the earth
Has changed its shape so many times
That water must now be

Our only symbol of those truths
That never change. The fickle earth
Has broken all its pledges. Now
I dare not trust its firmer floor.

But men prefer familiar earth
And laugh as if I were a fool
When I denounce its blatant lies.
What other listeners should I seek

To warn in vain? My oracles
Must now pursue their course while I,
Watching the fields in which their seeds
Are cast, may never reap their fruit.

My book of dreams has been unsealed.
As I read it, I'm now free to speak
Of joy for many moons: the sands
Have sipped the waters of my woes

And the deserts of love are blossoming
Wherever I wept. I trace
The calculations of my great content
On the virgin stretches of the sand

And add the sum of all delight.
Using the stars as counting-beads
For muttered calculations, I confer
A prize upon a statue, one of those

That imitate our wisdom best
Without partaking of our sorrows.
Who scoffs? My runes and riddles conceal
Only my laughter, a secret for fools.

My joy is clearer than the sky
That flaps its gonfalons of blue
Above our heads, more vast than the sea
That seals the boundary of these sands!

The pure spears of the sunlight fall
Upon the silent sands
And their midday union marks
A pause in all eternity.

Paris, 1927

THE PROPHET DELIVERED

for Carlos Suares

I.

I have witnessed timeless terrors in the depths of a mystic night and my head has been a wheel in a mazelike machinery of dreams.

When I return from the ocean of my dreams the sweat of an inspired past drips from my brow and my hair is matted with the blood of a womblike night.

In my dreams I have heard voices from another world. I have been a harp in the hands of demons and have been the flute through which the breath of demons flows.

I have shattered the skies, my fists have hammered new rhythms into eternity, and I have been

the divine rebel of space. My head has been a drum in the erratic hands of time and I have felt music,

the music of lost hopes and of revolt, the music of living death and of dead life, the music of eternity beaten upon my brain.

I have felt my brain like a fish in an endless ocean and I have felt that ocean in my brain.

I have counted the stars and found them too few; I have counted the drops of the ocean and not found them enough to satisfy my thirst;

and I have built palaces of smoke and found them too enduring for my desire of eternal action.

I have been the priest of my own religion and the god of my own religion,

and been for myself the rock that gives birth to a stream of self-love and self-hate.

I have invented new sins like flowers in the night, deathless sins that find no punishment worthy of their magnitude.

I have been a jewel to myself and a source of life in the deserts of solitude; I have been an angel and a demon, a bible and a book of vice, eternal and ephemeral, and I have been the all-in-all to every moment of my thought.

There have been no boundaries to my power, no tears to repent my errors, no echoes to the rumbling of my blasphemies.

25

The memory of my prodigious hands is like green waters that flow on the surface of the elements, and the shadow of my deeds is like the smoke of a burning city.

My hands have held the ocean and the stars: the ocean with all its ships, the stars with all their centuries of space; and I have been Leviathan that swallowed eternity.

I have found no present, no past and no future; I have abolished the walls of time and my senses have been a deliberate contradiction of my mind.

I have counted my words and they were innumerable; I ceased to count them and they ceased to be;

and now I count them again, and their numbers are no longer sufficient.

I have found a cross of words to exorcise each ghost; I have found an ocean of sleep whose waves are boundless in their bounties of oblivion;

and my head has cooled its fever in the waters of dreams.

My flowing hair has been the current of the encircling ocean, and my breath has driven the clouds across the sky.

I cannot count the forms of my soul and I cannot foretell all its delights:

I have been the conjuror of the elements and from the endless warfare of my soul I have saved

those words that are my soul.

My words are a rhetoric of discontent.

Priest of revolt seated upon the brink of the world, speech of the unknown gods,

I,

lost emblem of my own soul, city of rotting words, I, ruin of a rotting tongue,

I, endless flow of words, I, flower of the night, breast of the earth, I, nothing of nothing,

I, dust of the Almighty, Immortal juggler of words and of revolt,

I bruise my fists against a glorious rock,

my fiery fists that have grasped

the eternal concubinage of the skies.

I have slept in caverns of time and drunk the wine of space,

and now I come to record my dreams and the hallucinations of my soul.

26

I have seen gulfs and peaks, stars and the yawning void,
and my limbs have been cramped by the drugs of my
dreams.
And now I come but no longer know
why I have come.

I have come in the storm and I am the storm and the breath
of the storm that breaks itself against itself.
I have come and my heart has found no heart and my lips no
words to speak I have come and my words are lost I have
come.
And the beat of my heart is the drum of my coming but the
words of my coming have lost their sense and their sound in my
mouth.
I have come and I crush the bones of the dawn I have come
and I am the lord of the dawn and the lord of space and the
lord of my heart and the lord of lost words.
I have come and have lost the tracks and time of my coming
and forgotten the source of my coming and the aim of my
coming.
I have come from the soft green twilight of the sea and the
cruel red depths of the sun I have come in a storm of words and
I break the black iron bars of death I have come.
I have come and have found the statues of death in the
temple of death and the tomb of lost words and have felt in my
flesh the claws of life and on my neck the breath of life and on
my hands the blood of the sun I have come and have drunk
the blood of the sun and the wine of space and the waters of
death and the honey of love and the poison of hate.
I have come in the flow of an endless love I have come in the
breath of the beasts of the wind and I am the wind and its
beasts.
I have come and my breath is a warning of the past and a
memory of the future and my mind is a leaf in the wind and I
am the wind
and my brain is a drum which my own hands beat
I have come and have found the threshold of life and the
pillars of life and the wings of life I have come in a tempest of
life I have come.

Crucified upon the cruel sky,
my hands
are pierced with nail-like stars, my hair
is stretched on looms of night and plucked
like strings on astral harps;

and in my brutal agony I find
the birth of words,
and in my halting breath I feel
the birth of worlds:

and first you see
the swift movements of wings, of claws, of fins,
and then there come
before the multitude of nameless things,
women and the silken flowers that bloom between their
thighs,
philosophers and the beards of words that grow around their
lips,
warriors and the scent of battles in their matted arm-pits,
and angels, half-man, half-beast.

And who are you
who come thus in their midst?
and who are you
whose breath is like the steam of bubbling cauldrons or the
breath of unknown beasts of dreams?

In your tracks is the scent of a strange sweat
and the saliva of your mouth leaves a new scent in the sky,
and who are you
who have arisen in the midst of portents and prodigies?

And then there come
the leaves of our desires, the deathless loves of trees, the
flowers that are flesh,
and then there come
the cloud-white women of the firmament;
and the philosopher with the geometrical methods of his
wisdom like a crown set on his head,

and the dark warrior strong in the blood-scented presence of
his spear,
and the nameless things revolving in the sky like insects in the
pathless grass.

Before my eyes:
the birth of worlds,
in the chaos of their birth,
in the tumult of their birth,
who are you?

The sounds of force break paths through space around my
face the bristling spears of sound abound and pierce my ears
my eyes are torn by shafts of dawn a taste of steel and steel-like
cries now binds my tongue with cruel bands my raw hands
clasp trumpets of brass the dust of travel in my nostrils and my
hands my hands that cling to iron bars of space
ah fiery sun and howling machinery of life!
And you here in its midst?

Where are the gentle scents sight and touch of love in this
chaos of sounds:
an infinite pounding of my senses and the endless hammering
of murderous songs?
And you, the monster of my dreams, whose scaly breast,
whose wings
whose terrifying eyes whose breath whose burning breath
and you
whose claws whose breath whose burning body is pressed
against my own,
and you here in its midst?

The stench of your scaly body in the night!
And in the whirling firmament the symbols of a new-born
world:
philosophers, warriors, women, and the nameless things that
fade.

III.

for Georges Neveux

And suddenly you appeared
between the orbits of two moons;
I could not find your eyes, your hands,
the symbols of your love and power,
and your shadow fell across the last excesses of the day.
Your hands were lost
and as I fumbled in the fold of night
I found no proof of all your powers;
your head your eyes were lost
and in the waters of the night
I found no lights of love.
There had been eyes
there had been senses like five fingers
through which the elements flowed to your brain,
but where are they?

Tell me, Lord
of writhing darkness and of marble nights,
tell me the secret of your endlessness, show me the cavern
of your birth where darkness lifts adoring hands
around your luminous hidden head.
Where do you hide, you in whose limp grasp
the stars burst into scarlet flowers, in whose soft gaze
the moon glows like a milk-white horse?
Sinister and frequent visitor of my dreams,
companion of my loneliness and bird
of prey that hovers above the wastes of contemplation. . .
My hands are pressed against my ears and my cries are like
silken robes tossed by the winds . . . .

Oh bird,
giant bird of madness and emblem of dark prophecy!

I dream again of hands, a maze
of struggling hands and some are weak and idle,
others strong and seem to seek to tear the world apart,
grasp at a fleeting cloud.
I see a profile

and limbs whose forms are cast upon the clouds
and a hand that holds a golden flower before my eyes,
and the skies are full of breasts and the earth exhales a breath
of love;
but where am I
amidst all these mysterious limbs?
There are limbs in the sky and the breasts of vestals in the
dawn
but where am I
where are
my hands? O dark rock breaking the tumultuous yellow
waves of dawn,
Lord of night let your hands
be lanterns in my vast night let your eyes
be shining oceans let your limbs
be black marble columns to support the dome of my night!

These skies, these endless embraces of the loving heavens
these clouds in which the night
gives birth to its own darkness, these pale moons, and you
seated in their midst!
Your feet
trace circles in the air
your hands
are plucking the blood-red stars
Your hair
is trailing in the tangled fields
Your limbs
are wound around the nebulae of space;

but where am I?

Your limbs that rise like pillars to the stars your head
that finds its tomb its pyramid in space
your hands
that flow like greedy waters in the hidden caverns of the sky
your hair
your body that writhes like seaweed in the depths
your hands your hands . . .

but where am I?

Your hands swift birds that swoop
out of the pious sky your hands
that grasp the writhing snakes of night your hands
a torch in the night the torch for my path . . . .

but where am I?

IV.

Where are the hands that surged
from darkness in the dismal twilight of my dreams?
Where are the feet
that trampled the writhing paths of night?

The linen robes of evening fluttered in the wind
ennobled with a crest of sperm
and clouds like limbs of women drooped towards the
tree-tops
when I came
to those regions where a woman slung between the pits of
Heaven and Hell
gave birth to the tree of life.

In the shadow of rubies and emeralds
beneath the tall black masts of death
at the foot of the tree, I found
what I sought, a tangle of writhing forms
like rotting carrion, from which I plucked
shapes and names, a new world
of birds and beasts for the tree.

I wrought the beauty of their songs, I wove
the embrace of foliage around their nests,
I shaped the beasts that live in the tree
and the roots too of the tree
that fed on the blood of the womb.

Madonna of darkness
Earth of the tree of life
Source of all love whose eyes
are suns, bright with the fires of life,

I too have come to eat the fruit
of your forbidden tree
I too have felt the burning embrace
of chaos and confusion and the cold sweat of creation on my
limbs
When I gave birth to worlds of words,
to lands and cities and their populations, to fields and factories
and homes
to beasts and machines, as I kneaded my words and moulded
them like clay,
Emulating nature or a god in my work,
in the beginning, with a word
like a seed that burst and gave birth
to heavens and oceans, to fabulous beasts of dreams,
to the new and the old, the real and the unreal,
all born of my mind, a womb of dreams.

Paris, 1928

33

LETTERS TO A MURDERER

I.

Where you rested your hand there rose
the ghost of flames leaping
across the dark and silken ocean, hearts
that bled and faded into the heavy sky.
And in the shadow of your hand

there were ships and towers where the sea's lips met the earth's,
and there was music, and waves that rolled like dark cloaks round the loins
of horses that vanished into the waters. And when I looked again
there were the vanishing tracks of alien feet in the fiery sands,
and the towers had burst into purple blossoms that tore the sky
with the thrust of their birth.

Where have my eyes
deciphered more cryptic messages
than on the key-board of the singing sea?

The silent shells of time
lay shattered on the shore and in the midst
of strange wreckage, broken instruments, tangled tackle and seaweed like tortured veins
I found an abandoned hand,
and fragments of a broken knife-blade and a skein of hair
and a metal box that flashed with stones like stars and opened silently,
revealing a treasure of human teeth.
Where had I been
since your hand left its scent upon my shoulder,
since the night fell across my eyes, since the sun revealed to me
the death of fish dissolving in its slow embrace?
Where had I been:
lost in the geometry of the lines that join our feet to northern

stars
  and suspend the circling birds from the weary sun?

  You know the name
  of the woman who lived amongst trees, lifting her hands like
a broken pitcher to the clouds,
  you know why the cruel birds circled around her head,
tearing her lank black hair,
  and you never said
  where I would find paths to lead me back to her feet
  and the scent of her presence like a handkerchief waved in
the night.
  And it was your hand
  that let loose the hounds and broke the seals of sleep,
  your hand that held a burning cross in the night-sky
  so that it shone against heaving hills in the turmoil of an
earthquake.
  And you knew the names of the leaves
  that guilty men chew to forget their crimes
  and that pour sleep like a balm on the brow of weary
travellers,
  you knew the forests where the lonely woman lives
  and gathers these leaves as she waits
  for the quiet sound of my feet on the virgin soil.

  And now your hand
  has left no shadow but the fragrant scent of blood
  that evaporates and soon
  must fade.

II.

  Your hand can force the iron hold
  of every spell. Your power
  can emulate that of the night.
  The mandragora of my dreams
  must cease to flower in devilries
  and hallucinations, half-plant,
  half-man, when your hand at last
  sets a boundary to any world
  that I devise and then destroy.

35

Your will must be a light
that leads me to self-knowledge when,
in the gloom of chaos, in the depths
of every ocean, I still find
the watchful presence of your eyes.

Your eyes can drift in currents
of vision like two fish
lost in the sea's embrace. I dreamed
of horses once. Their silken necks
rippled like sea-weed in the drift.

The stallions of my dream are drowned.
Their nostrils, snorting with desire,
have dissolved in another darkness
that brings in turn a dream of hands
with all the swift delights of love.

Your head can sow the seeds of death.
Its grip can strangle the pale dawn.
The shadow of your hand can break
the spell of night, your fist like a rock
that marks the frontier of the night.

PRAYERS AT DAWN

Ah, burning towers of dawn,
torn entrails of the sky
borne on the spears of day.

The blood of vanquished night,
and the dirges of nightingales,
mourning night, now like the carcase
of a brittle insect, while the dawn
comes with its horses snorting in the wind.

And the sun, unholy fires
forbidden fruit of the sky, our hands
stretched out towards the rising sun,
our hands like votive offerings,
the garland of our hands upraised
towards the rising sun.

And I would grasp this burning fruit,
apple of light, with greedy hands
reaching for the forbidden sun:

SEA LOST SOUL

For Harold Salemson

Lions of sand with soft flowing manes
ripple beside the boneless sea
where the grey wind and relentless rains
drown my dim footprints, feet that flee.

There my lost hands have often sought
tendrils of time and acanthus leaves
around the sea's silver goblet wrought.
Metallic, the sea for ever grieves

my dreamship that sank, broken masts, torn sails,
and all souls lost in a tempest where
the blood-red sun roused the killer-whales
whose lowing can mimick the wind's despair.

ARRIVAL IN THE CITY OF DREADFUL NIGHT

for Georgette Camille

THUS WE CAME

and we came into the city
black monster beneath a scarlet sky
two small men dragging
the long chain of our weary tracks
we crawled into the filthy gloom we crawled
as into the womb of an operatic whale
the blood-scented darkness caressing
our limbs and the walls of houses
leaning menacing staring

THUS WE CAME

into the city where the weary men
bore olives and the scent of bitter wine
in the basket of their armpits

THUS WE CAME

spider-like suspended on our tracks
into the womb into the tomb

THUS WE CAME

POEM

hammers of bronze beat
time for the cities from
clock-towers
          throbbing of
feet in muddy streets to a
clock-rhythm sways
             heads
nod
  TIME
    two three four five six seven eight nine ten eleven
TIME
    dies where are the
beasts that breathe steam through
steel mouths shrilly the
curling smoke-clouds like
black stallions where the
roar of cities
         sudden
silence of cities time has
stolen their stones their steel their
clamor in death.

SOLAR MYTH

swift clatter of feet on
echoing stairs opening like
blossoms   hands reach out
grasping the heights and
in the eyes gleam
fires of fortune flowering
by chance

       the walls drip
clammy murder   still the feet
hasten up the stairs seeking
heights the heights or chariots
to carry them heavenwards

the sun's blare bursts the sky
the eyes wither seared to
wrinkled petals   and the
chariot falls
        falls

into the ocean scattering
death-rays on the blood-stained earth

POEM

for Mrs. Edgar Tindall

I
came I came from nowhere
driven on to nothing in
wind and sounds of brazen
music unable to clutch at
bars of space I came just as a
rushing of winds just as an
eagle swooping down into
jaws of void an insect
crawling out of darkness growing
larger as the light of day grows
brighter on its steel wings I
came just as an athlete
leaping from brink to brink through
boundless space I came as
thunder rolls loud and
louder until it
stops but
I can
not
stop

FOR ALICE NIKITINA

Snow awaits footprints.
Silence awaits sound.

I came into the snow.
                    My feet print
tracks in snow, my mind weaves
words in silence : foot-prints,
· sudden swooping birds of
presence let loose in
emptiness, stray cards
scattered on white tables of
snow.

                    The snow sank
          out of silence into
          blur of ghost-voices.

Out of my feet,
track-children; ghost-children of
sound out of my
mind.

                    There is no
snow, no snow but this
printing of tracks in
emptiness; no silence but this
weaving of ghost words.
Tracks that lead back to my
feet, words leading back to my
mind.

               No silence . . . .
                    I came into
          silence. When I came there was
          no silence where once silence,

tracks where once no tracks;
snow still, but snow changed.

43

Silence alone died
killed by ghost voices.

AVATAR

*"La treizième revient: c'est toujours la
première ... "*   Gérard de Nerval

You came,
    but not the same:
a tentative smile,
    dim eye,
and why
this wealth of words among
the wiles of your smile,
    and why
the barbed tip of your tongue
tearing apart your words?
You came
    again—
the same
but not the same
    name—
you again:
you spoke of trees   leaves   clouds   birds
    and left
the world
    bereft
as each cloud unfurled
    its widowhood
You again
    where your shadow last stood.

Prose Prose
(1929-1932)

THE NEW REALITY

First English and American
Surrealist Manifesto

*One cannot knowingly revolt without first
having tried and perhaps failed to conform.*
—Antonin Artaud (in conversation)

It has so far escaped the notice of most critics that modernism in literature is no longer new: there are already two generations in modernism: one which has established itself as a tradition, and one which is still in revolt. Many writers of the first generation, the Sitwells and Harold Acton, are beginning to be rather *vieux jeu*; all the great modernists are of this older generation; Eliot, Miss Stein, James Joyce, Cummings, Ezra Pound, Archibald MacLeish, Laura Riding, Marianne Moore, Robert Graves, and the Sitwell trinity. All these writers, after much experimenting, have achieved their aims: Eliot has found purity of style and a perfect classicism; Miss Stein has produced entirely abstract prose; James Joyce in his new work has attained the vigor of style which always was his objective and is creating the new mythology which was his ideal; Cummings is swiftly becoming a purely typographical poet; Ezra Pound's cantos are the fruit of years of experimenting in every style of verse; MacLeish's new poem, *Hamlet*, marks his return to metaphysical poetry; Miss Riding, Miss Moore, and Robert Graves, intending to be as dry and technical as possible, can be compared only to some very interesting form of dust; Miss Sitwell's last poem, *Metamorphosis*, is a seventeenth-century costume-play, and Sacheverell Sitwell, having put Keats, Gongora, and the lesser-known Elizabethans into the same mixing bowl, is no longer a modernist. Nearly all these writers have ceased to innovate, and the newcomer in literature finds it useless to follow them. He can continue the literary chain where they have dropped it. The Sitwells he can dismiss as mere antiquarians who, like Beddoes, will interest students of literature as an anachronism. He must therefore choose the other great modernists as his starting-point.

A starting-point is a point that one leaves behind; in literature one revolts against a starting-point. The chief quality of most of these writers is precision; therefore one revolts against precision, since precision cannot be carried any farther. For precision is the heirloom of the younger generation; every young modernist poet begins with precision and can be as logical or illogical as he likes; he has complete mastery of expression and knows exactly where to place each word. He must therefore revolt by bringing an element of chance into his poetry. This element of chance is surréalisme.

Surréalisme is not a new aestheticism of lilies, caviar, lipsticks, flowing ties, etc., but a revolt against aestheticism. The surréaliste poet does not write sonnets but prefers to say:

the small bird is seen to be superfluous at night.

He does not believe in beauty, but in dreams or Crispin Quirk or any other thing or person that contains some element of chance or of the miraculous.

There are moments in the life of every true poet when poetry is no longer a geranium in a flower-pot on his window-sill and beauty no longer wears a capital B like a green dress from Paquin; but when beauty is an accident and poetry an inexplicable miracle. The words come naturally with the speed of a murderous wind or of barley-sugar disappearing into the mouth of a small boy in his dreams; and their meaning is no longer a purpose but an accident. The writer is no longer a person but an accident. Everything is an accident. The poem may be beautiful when finished, and it may be ridiculous and comical. It may be necessary to change it, and the poem may be complete as it stands. Inspiration comes down from the clouds of dreams, suspended on the unexpected parachute of a new reality. A table is no longer a spade (all tables are spades) but becomes the battlefield on which will take place the terrible union of the male pen and the female paper that rushes upwards to meet its mate.

What is reality

a tooth-brush, a potato, a check-book, a small bird, an illusion?

Reality is the unpoetic state of mind. But there is another reality: the new reality of poetry. Poetry is not a purpose; poetry is the poem once written. One does not write poetry; one has written poetry. For according to this new reality poetry is no longer an art but the result of the writer's contact with the new reality, and with its messenger, the new muse.

Often in the past poets have been visited by this new muse, but instead of recognizing her nudity as the very incarnation of beauty or poetry (both with and without capital letters), have forced her into a corset of hexameters and made her look like any other muse. The surréaliste poet accepts her as she comes; he has learned to distinguish her from Miss Turnip, the muse of the "genuine feeling for nature," and Miss Prism, the muse of the "sensitive yet deeply philosophical poet," and Calliope-Io, the garden statue who dictates "fantasy and truth" to Miss Sitwell. This new muse is different from all the other old maids of Parnassus, Montparnasse, and Chelsea; she learned precision and style in T. S. Eliot's school, where Joyce occasionally lectured on vigor; then she went to a finishing-school in Paris, where she learned to dream like Lautréamont and to despise Cocteau and the Sitwells. She has chosen Joyce, Eliot, MacLeish, and Ezra Pound as her English masters.

She is as changeable as Proteus. To Robert Desnos she often appears in rhyme; to Fargue she sings sadly in a minor key; to Georges Neveux she dictates melodious verses which should be read aloud upon the house-tops of a mysterious pagan city; to Jules Supervielle she appears with many of the attributes of Miss Prism (but with none of the faults of Miss Prism). And it is this same muse who dictated *The Waste Land* to Eliot, the *Cantos* to Pound, and the *Hamlet* to MacLeish. For surréalisme is not her only occupation and aim; she existed long before the surréalistes began to obey her; she revealed herself in her purest form to Rimbaud, Lautréamont, and was finally accepted by a whole generation of young poets in Paris. She is the only living muse. She has never heard of Cocteau, Miss Sitwell, Masefield, Mr. Alfred Noyes, Paul Geraldy, Ella Wheeler Wilcox, Wyndham Lewis, Rita Francis Mosscockle, Lord Tennyson, and Maurice Rostand. She does not visit Miss Stein, Miss Laura Riding, Miss Marianne Moore, Mr. Cummings, and all the other latter-day saints of technique. Her parachute does not often descend upon English soil; for she is terrified of the poet laureate, the censor, the Conservative Association, buy British goods, empire day, do your Christmas shopping early, the Queen's doll's house, sales on now, why not wear the boston garter.

There is no muse there are no muses there never was a muse there never were any muses. A muse is a state of mind that produces art. The new muse is a new state of mind which produces new art. *Twice two is four*. But this new muse is not

51

new this state of mind is not new. It has always existed but has never yet been cultivated, but has never yet been an accepted institution like the hexameter, the sonnet, the triolet, and that eminently poetical object the corset.

This new reality is the reality of dreams and of dark rooms filled with the buzzing light of ultra-violet rays; it is the reality of red sunsets on dark seas, where whales call to their mates in the tones of an apocalyptic primadonna; the reality of advertisements read backwards and of umbrellas blown away by the wind to mysterious horizons beyond the house-tops; the reality of walking-sticks that become snakes and snakes that become hair and hair that rises vertically towards the sun so as to form new rays from the earth to the sun. Birds are suspended from the sun by the long golden chains of their burning songs; birds dream of disappointed experience and sing in their sleep when they hear of the death of the word LOVE.

This is the new reality: the reality of the night, of the brilliant sunlight, the reality of dreams, hallucinations and the prophecies announced in the singing heat of noon; the reality of visions which later are interpreted as religions, philosophies, and metaphysics; the reality of symbols before they have been proven to be symbols; of words that spring living from the womb of Time. The birds dream darkly and the prophet sees his own profile reflected upon a passing cloud; the trees turn in spirals toward the singing sun and a curious small dark animal appears from among the thick jungle-grass of the infinite. This is the new reality this animal is the new reality.

The new reality, the new muse, the new state of mind ignore technique because it is technique. They appear only to the poet whose knowledge of technique is sufficient; many poets pretend to have been initiated into this new reality and say that their deformed prose is the poetry of the new reality. Beware of the charlatans of the new reality. For the new reality, like biscuits, caramels, and many other excellent products, can be counterfeited by cunning swindlers. *Se méfier des contrefaçons.*

Oxford, 1928

PREFACE TO AN AUTOBIOGRAPHY

At this point in his life, the author of the following pages felt an imperative urge to introduce himself to his few anonymous friends, his possible public of admirers, by means of a diary, an autobiographical duplicate of his life.

The above-mentioned author, R., has never existed. He has not yet been born. His only existence has so far been that of a wraith, an exhalation of the minds of other beings, a being whose future presence was, as it were, anticipated by a group of other beings who still believed in the power of second sight, not yet realizing that they were only being deluded by their own over-fertile imaginations. In fact, their faith in R.'s existence was such that he was finally forced to believe in it himself and to accept it as absolute and undeniable gospel-truth, which his every observation of objective phenomena invariably tended to corroborate. In short, the author of these pages was a myth, a spirit conjured out of the imagination of a few other spirits who, losing all control over their own creature, were unable to exorcise it, forgot the only formula whereby it could be relegated to the limbo to which it more naturally belonged, and were forced to let it live, in the hope that it would live and let live, or that the problem would solve itself of its own accord, that the ghost would be inspired to recite this formula which they had forgotten, to exorcise itself and commit suicide. Meanwhile, out of a certain sense of responsibility towards this child of their own dreams, they continued to feed it daily on their thoughts, lest it starve and take it into its head to punish them for their negligence by haunting them after its death, or far worse, bring them into discredit in the eyes of others, by proclaiming to all and sundry their meanness and lack of natural parental affections. Thus they were never able to forget the present author's existence, nor to behave suddenly as if he were no longer there, but, since the universe had chosen to expand in this direction and could now no longer be persuaded to contract, were forced to keep him perpetually in mind, letting him live by a sort of fixed commission on their own existence, consecrating to his upkeep a regular percentage of their conscious thoughts and even of their dreams, allowing him to continue, in peace, his parasitic existence. Gradually, however, owing to the healthy nourishment thus meted out to him in his infancy and growing-years, this strange and whimsical spirit, R., was able to provide himself, out of his own savings, with a tangible body of his own, by a process analogous to that of crystallization in a super-saturated solution of those thoughts of others which were left over after he had taken his daily sustenance. The different elements of his physical being were borrowed: a nose which one ancestor had imagined, eyes from the dreams of another, limbs from the desires of a third, a body from the various imaginings of various people, a face, a navel, and—but how he managed this no one could understand—even a soul. In one respect alone did R. fail to give himself his due: he was completely unable to provide himself with an individual "ego" to command, like a field-marshal, the complicated *corps d'armée* of his numerous component parts. This last could only be provided by experience, by the actions of his component parts in the surrounding world, their reactions to this world and to each other: wherefore R. now writes invariably in the third person singular, being totally incapable of pronouncing, writing, or even conceiving the first, which denotes the consciousness of an individual subjective ego. R., however, still hopes that the writing of these pages may in some way help him solve this last problem of his own entity; for a problem it certainly is, as this absence of an individual consciousness, this privation in his entity, remains a distinct barrier to all conversation, a great social disadvantage and an impediment in his relationships with other individuals. This same peculiarity in R.'s character probably also accounts for his distressing obscurity as an author, in spite of his undeniable talent. And one would not be far wrong in guessing that it is for this same reason that R. is as yet unmarried; for, before loving or fathering any others, R. must first learn to love and father himself.

The author of these pages is at the present moment deeply puzzled. He is wondering from whom, of his many friends and begetters, the above-written words have been borrowed. For, had they not been borrowed—that is to say, if their source were not only virtually untraceable, but absolutely nonexistent—they themselves would never have come to be printed here on this page. The author of these remarks hereby wishes to declare himself totally incapable of the parthenogenesis which such an act of pure creation would entail. These words and the thoughts that they express have obviously been borrowed from somewhere or someone. Otherwise they would not now be here. In the beginning was the word; then came the so-called author.

The so-called author hereby wishes to disclaim all responsibility other than syntactical or prosodic for the existence or meaning of these words. He accuses his creators, his readers, or the words themselves; but he fails to see how he himself can in any way be held responsible for the existence of these words or the sense of these pages. These words and the thoughts that they express have been inherited by the so-called author from the generations of his creators and of the creators of his creators; they are, in a way, his own brothers; or have always existed with an absolute and separate existence of their own, independent of the various human processes of heredity and begetting. R. tends likewise to believe that his readers can even less justifiably be held responsible for the words that they read and for the conclusions that they draw from these words than he himself for the words that he writes and the sense that these words express. More probably, no one is ever responsible for anything, but everything always responsible for everyone.

At various moments in his life, if life it can be called, R., the author of these lines, if author there must be, has tended to believe, on the grounds of his own individual experience, that there never was any such thing as individual existence: in fact, that individual consciousness, together with its corollaries of individual experience and existence, is probably little more than an optical illusion, a dream in which matter sees itself duplicated, in which matter watches itself watching itself, a hallucination, a mirage, a myth. And at other moments the author has felt equally attracted to the theory that individual human consciousness is a disease of matter, a local irritation, an auto-intoxication; in fact, that the human race is a sort of disease of the planet on which it exists, a rash which has irrationally appeared and would probably likewise soon disappear, leaving this planet as healthily unconscious of individual existence as any other. Certainly both these theories seem to account fairly satisfactorily for the author's own existence; for which reason the author now submits them to his public's approval.

Let each one of the author's readers now imagine himself author of this autobiographical preface. Let each one of them imagine that he, or she, is writing it at this moment, or has only just written this meagre account of his, or her, own individual existence. Let them all at the same moment imagine that they are writing it now. Let the pen which is writing these words be impelled by the individual consciousness of each one of these various individuals, all summarized in the one person of the present above-mentioned author. Let the author of these words cease to exist except as a function of the readers for whom he is writing. The author of these words has ceased to exist. Readers, you are the authors of these pages. Being utterly exorcised, the above-mentioned author, R., can now at last in all safety pronounce the possessive pronoun of the first person singular:

Hypocrite lecteur! mon semblable, mon frère!

London, 1932

Prose Poems
(1929-1973)

THE RISE AND FALL OF THE ROMAN REPUBLIC: How Rome was built in a day.

for Paul Bowles

An antlike crowd had been marching past us for several hours, it now seemed, though the diminutive marchers remained barely discernible beneath a bristling umbrella of banners, insignia and trophies that they bore aloft, as if to conceal from their eyes the incestuous wedlock of the drifting clouds, which continued to copulate and multiply in the blue sky, driven by a high wind under the complacent gaze of the imperturbably hermaphroditic sun. The municipal police, in dark blue uniforms adorned with golden badges which proclaimed them servants of this ambiguous ball of fire, were meanwhile kept busy, gigantically tall and stout men with the placid and smooth countenances of eunuchs, channeling the procession as it progressed almost aimlessly along the city's main arteries with its head so close to its own tail that nobody could tell who was a leader or who was a straggler and where it proposed, if at all, to go.

But the wind suddenly descended with the impact of a hurricane from the higher regions of the sky and its destructive assault was immediately followed by a heavy downpour of hail and of ice-cold rain. Within a few minutes, the avenue beneath our balcony was deserted. In a flurry like that of autumn leaves in the first wintry gale, the crowd had scattered, as if literally blown away. Then a huge mass of water that had mysteriously gathered strength and momentum in the ominous hills above the city descended on it like a tidal wave and swept down the avenue towards the harbor, washing everything away and leaving in its wake an empty plain where only scattered débris, the flotsam and jetsam of catastrophe, could still reveal the extent of the destruction which we had just witnessed and miraculously survived.

How had we managed, Remus and I, to find ourselves at the right moment and quite by chance on this balcony of the only building which, as far as we could see, had withstood the impact of both the cyclone and the flood? We now stood side by side, alone as we overlooked a vast expanse of mud-flats, scarcely even able to remember how, only a few moments earlier, we had been peacefully watching from our balcony the entire population of a crowded but doomed metropolis marching past

59

us in an aimless and endless procession which might otherwise have continued forever. Somewhat apprehensively, we now withdrew from our balcony into the silent and deserted building. There we found our way, without any difficulty, down the stairs and out into the empty mud-flats that surrounded us.

But these, as if awakening from a nightmare, began to revive in an orgy of vernal activity. Like green obscenities, viscous and phallic plants, some of them soon as tall as trees, were sprouting out of the wet earth all around us. In the shade that they supplied from the midday heat of the sun, flushed animals of fire, still glowing beneath their cinder-grey fleeces, began busily to pursue and court each other and even to mate in the clearings of the forest where we now found ourselves wandering. Ahead of us, leading us on to an unknown destination, fresh human footprints caught our attention in the mud that was already becoming dry and hard as the heat increased even in the steaming shade of the new-born forest.

We followed these tracks through the forest and into the ominous hills, where they abruptly came to an end on the summit of one of the low foothills, as if our invisible guide, whoever he might have been, had been lifted here bodily into the sky rather than swallowed up by the earth, since we could find on the ground no trace or scar of any recent chasm that might have sealed itself of its own accord or healed like a wound after welcoming its victim into its gaping depths. But had an eagle or a chariot of fire then borne our vanished guide aloft into the sky that, beyond the green canopy of trees, was now cloudless as far as the eye could see? We could find no scattered feathers, such as a gigantic bird might have lost as its desperate human prey struggled to free himself from its talons, nor could we detect any tracks of burning wheels in the scorched mud, nor any singed leaves in the few trees that surrounded the spot where our lost guide's last footprints were clearly marked in the dry mud.

Whoever our guide might have been—I suggested Elijah while Remus opted for Ganymede—, he had failed, before vanishing, to notify the responsible authorities—but were there any here?—of his imminent change of address. Unless a new miracle occurred, we had no means of discovering who had led us here, nor why.

An event of this nature nevertheless seemed to deserve some

kind of memorial or cenotaph, some empty tomb that we would dedicate to the memory of an utterly anonymous being whom we had never seen, but whose disappearance now left us bereft, puzzled and mourning. Instead of accepting his mysterious absence as a grim warning of the fate that might well be awaiting us too, and consequently confessing immediately our more or less imaginary sins in order to prepare ourselves for the very worst, perhaps even for a Last Judgment that might also never occur, we decided then and there to commemorate what seemed to have failed to happen, I mean our final meeting with our guide, or rather his disappearance or his reabsorption into a state of non-existence or of non-happening, by building here in his honor some more useful monument than the customary cenotaph; in fact a luxury hotel that would be able to accomodate in comfort all future pilgrims to this historic site, dedicated from now on as a shrine to the Eternal Solution of Continuity.

As soon as we had agreed on this plan, the canopy of foliage of the trees beneath which we were resting parted above us to allow a sailing-ship, fully rigged and with all sails spread to the winds, to descend majestically from the blue lagoon of the sky and come peacefully to anchor, a few yards ahead of us, on the green sward of a clearing, as if this were its normal port of call. From its deserted main deck, where we could see no other man or officer, a lone young sailor clambered briskly down a rope ladder to the ground, holding in his mouth what appeared to be a manilla envelope. Without any hesitation, he hastened towards us, saluted us smartly, handed us his missive, saluted us again, then sprinted back towards his ship, which sailed off again into the sky as soon as he had returned to its main deck.

Remus stood there, wide-eyed and open-mouthed in amazement as he watched the schooner sail away through the tree-tops into the sky, but fumbling undecidedly the envelope that he held in his hands, as if not daring to open it. I grabbed it from him, tore it open and began to read aloud its contents to my intermittently identical twin:

"Dear putative sons of the legendary she-wolf,
                                        I am sure
you have not yet found time to prepare a detailed plan for my proposed memorial as well as an estimate of the cost of constructing it. But this should be the least of my

61

worries or indeed of yours. I now enclose a blank check on the Bank of the Holy Ghost, made out to the bearer. Tear it up in as many pieces as you can, scatter its fragments to the frivolous winds, and hope for the best. I can assure you, you will not be disappointed. Until further notice, I beg to remain your mysterious guide, neither Ganymede nor Elijah, neither Greek nor Tishbite, but still a bit of both."

The letter was signed, but with an utterly illegible signature. "You've invented every word of it," Remus exclaimed in anger, a doubting Thomas if there ever was one, as soon as I had finished reading him the text of the letter. To convince him of my good faith, I handed him the letter, so that he too would be able to read it. But I then saw, as I was handing it to him, the whole text become as scrambled and illegible as the signature when the paper reached his hand, then settle again in an entirely different but quite legible pattern, so that Remus now ready to me a different text:

"Dear Topsy and Turvy,
                                        I am sure that the plans and the estimate for the necessary repairs to my Eternal City are far beyond your abilities as architects, contractors or cost-accountants. I therefore enclose, for your personal use, a practical formula for extracting gold from sea-water. Go ahead and make a mint of money while I watch you and supervise your work from a safe distance. If you need any further instructions, consult my agents, the viscous trees and the cinder-grey beasts of smoldering fire. They are my emissaries and remain in constant contact with me, by means of a semaphoric communications system that permits exchange of information and views on subjects of topical interest between the machinery of their metabolism and my own encyclopaedic mind. Yours truly,

Again, the signature was illegible. "You see," Remus moaned, thoroughly discouraged, "now we have to work for a living, using the Pacific Ocean as a gold-mine and all of Australia and its central desert as our alchemist's crucible!"

I snatched the letter from his hand and read it again. Its text was again as I had first read it. This time, however, I noticed that an enclosure was pinned to it: the blank bearer-check on the Bank of the Holy Ghost, no practical alchemical formula for apprentice-sorcerers. To put an end to an otherwise fruitless discussion, I immediately tore the check up, according to the instructions contained in the letter as I had read it, and scattered the fragments of paper to the winds.

Wherever a piece of the torn check now fell, the earth opened up, revealing a pit of red clay like raw flesh; out of each one of these gaping wounds, a stream of bricks began to fly, as if on invisible conveyor-belts, and to assemble miraculously so as to form what we were soon able to recognize as the ramparts of a great walled city. We stood back and watched, amazed. As soon as one of the gates leading into the city was completed so that one could venture through it without being struck by any flying bricks, Remus and I decided to enter the city. But we halted in the shelter of the gateway. Beyond it, the bricks were still flying in all directions, like the waters of an enormous fountain, and assembling themselves of their own accord so as to produce in miraculous haste but with unhesitating precision, as if carrying out a mysteriously preconceived plan, the various buildings that would soon constitute an eternal city, built on seven hills and destined to survive for at least a thousand years all the depredations of nature, of man, of history and of decay.

For a long while we continued to watch the bricks fly all around us as they poured out of the earth in a frenzy of creative energy. Peals of satanic laughter could meanwhile be heard echoing in the bowels of the earth, wherever it had opened up so as to release the bricks from their secret subterranean kilns. As the city began at last to reveal its true plan and character, the color of the sunlight changed from the red of dawn or sunset to a golden yellow. Like clotted cream, the sunlight then settled on the brick surfaces of many of the buildings and soon solidified there, covering the reddish-brown walls with a fresh coating of what appeared to be curiously wrought or carved stucco or marble.

A loud clash of cymbals resounded beneath the vaulted sky to announce that the Eternal City was now fully built and ready to be occupied by its future citizens and visited by its future pilgrims. Remus and I then ventured into it, from the shelter of the gateway where we had stood watching, and we soon found our way, thanks to conveniently placed sign-posts all composed in the Church Latin of the distant future, through the metropolitan maze of streets to the summit of what we knew must be the city's Capitoline Hill. There a palace awaited us since we were, to all intents and purposes, the city's only human founders.

But we were no longer alone. From the noise that we now heard behind us, we realized that we were being followed, though at a respectful distance, by a crowd of marchers. As we reached the summit of the Capitoline Hill, I looked back just in time to see the leaders of the marching crowd emerge into the city, in the distance, through the gateway where we too had entered it. To me, the crowd seemed to be the same as the one we had watched earlier, from our balcony, before the hurricane and the flood had swept it away together with almost every trace of its all too ephemeral city. This new crowd seemed indeed to be bearing the same banners, insignia and trophies. Seen from such a distance, however, all crowds can well appear equally and identically antilike.

Remus and I had also been two small men, had anyone been watching us from the summit of the Capitoline Hill as we now watched this advancing crowd. We too had gradually grown taller as we progressed towards the Hill along the city's broad avenues, lined with all the historic monuments of its glorious future. Had we not been able to read, as we passed by them, the sign-posts that indicated the name of each building, informing us too of the year when it was destined to be built? We had thus discovered Baths of Diocletian and of Caracalla, an Arch of Titus and one of Vespasian, a Circus of Agrippina and one of Heliogabalus, a column of Tiberius and one of Nero, a Temple of the Vestal Virgins and a Theater of Messalina, all in the course of our progression towards the Capitoline Hill and of our ascension of its slope.

We had meanwhile found, on the summit of the Capitoline Hill, a temple-palace awaiting us, with a fine view of the whole city and up and down the valley of the Tiber. On the river's other bank, we could already discern Saint Peter's, the Vatican, and a number of hotels that stood there, ready to accommodate pilgrims. But we were left little time to wonder how so much had been providentially planned and built in so little time and in prevision of so many centuries of future history, for the porter of our Capitoline palace now came forward to greet us humbly and to hand us the keys of our official abode. In a formal speech, he announced that his name was Aeneas, and that the keys which he entrusted to us were also those of the Gates of Heaven.

The crowd which had followed us into the city had now reached the foot of the Capitoline Hill and appeared to be waiting there for some encouragement or permission to scatter and occupy the city. From a marble rostrum which had obviously been built there for some such purpose, I addressed the crowd and invited it to make itself at home as friends, Romans and countrymen.

Rome had indeed been built in a day, contrary to all expectations, and this was already the end of its first day. Remus and I withdrew into our Capitoline Palace, acclaimed enthusiastically by the crowd before it began to scatter peacefully. From a balcony overlooking the whole city, we then watched its thousands of lights appear one by one in the dusk as its innumerable palaces and more modest homes and tenements were occupied by all those whom we were destined to rule and to guide in the serious business of being Romans.

Paris, 1929

THROUGH THE NEEDLE'S EYE

for Paul Goodman

The sunlight, above the lawns and lagoons of the Park and over the lake-shore beyond, had assumed the golden quality of late afternoon that illuminates the classical landscapes of Claude Lorrain. I was just pointing this out to Paul as we left the Avenue that scintillated in a hot swirl of summer dust churned by constant traffic; we then plunged into the Park as into a cool green bath of dream.

We were discussing our friends Tom and Renzo. We thought that Tom, the eternal student, was deteriorating, which worried me. "Tom seems," I concluded "to have erred from the party-line of the angels in his pursuit of what he believes to be wisdom." Paul agreed with me. As for Renzo, the political scientist and antifascist exile, we felt that his renunciation of all theory in favor of what he believed to be practice was but a suicidal refusal to think.

"Yes," Paul added in his most diagnostic tone (such unerring insight into the sins and weaknesses of others!), "Tom is more interested in the formal and aesthetic aspects of wisdom than in the Good Life, where aesthetics and ethics are one. He is a rhetorician; all he wants is the skin-deep appearance of wisdom, just enough to earn him a quick but fleeting success."

Paul's evaluation of Tom perturbed me. Was I any better? Paul seemed to detect my anxiety, perhaps in my hesitancy to speak, and reassured me before I found time to express my doubts: "You, my dear Edouard, are more wise in your actions than in your words."

I felt relieved. While we walked ahead, Paul remarked that Renzo too was deteriorating. As a political scientist, he now allowed his bitter experience of politics in our age to discourage him so that he no longer really believed in the possible existence of a Good Society. But, if the Good Society cannot be achieved, there is no purpose in any science of politics, and if there is no purpose in science, there is no sense in rational thinking. So Renzo, though perhaps the most intellectual of us all, had renounced all rational thought in favor of a weirdly irrational preference for all that seemed to him immediately healthy and normal, at the merely animal level. "And that's why," Paul concluded, "Renzo now behaves as if, instead of the unusual

66

but real intellectual that he is, he were what he believes the average Italian-American laborer of poor immigrant stock to be, a fictional comic-strip character at best."

I agreed with Paul, but added that Renzo himself did not always seem satisfied with, or convinced by, his desired metamorphosis: "There's evidence of tension in him. No longer all that he's always been, he isn't yet what he wants to become. He's play-acting; and he has become the only audience that he's anxious to convince and actually convinces most rarely."

Again, Paul compared me to Renzo as he had already compared me to Tom: "You're more convincing. You employ your talents to convince others rather than yourself; your words generally seem very wise to the unwise and you certainly have rhetorical skill. But you nearly always speak the thoughts of others, rarely your own, and you illustrate your real wisdom obliquely, by saying what others want you to say—which relieves you from any involvement in profitless arguing—or what they least expect you to say. You satisfy or judiciously shock people, according to your mood, instead of arguing more directly. This too may be an effect of your gift of prudent action rather than for wise utterance. Your speech is a kind of action, a means to an end. Its wisdom is more often revealed in its objectives than in the principles that it seems to proclaim."

Paul again paused for a while and I remained silent, unable or unwilling to refute him. Then he added, as if to console me: "Still, you may be judged by your actions, which are wise, whereas Renzo's actions are unwise and Tom's words have only the superficial appearance of wisdom. Your actions reveal an understanding of the Good Life, so that you may yet enter into the Kingdom of Heaven."

We had reached the shore of the lagoon and were about to cross the wooden bridge to the island where the Japanese Tea-room usually stands, or at least always stood whenever either Paul or I had previously been there. Yet we were not surprised to discover now, from the middle of the hunched bridge, an entirely new panorama: a clustered Kremlin of domed and spired churches, built around lawns punctuated by ornamental groves and statues, and along canals hemmed in by long cloisters, episcopal palaces, baptistries, basilicas, Palladian libraries and monumental stone trophies representing allegorical victories or assumptions into heaven.

"This," Paul declared as he glanced at the maze of almost

stagnant water, time-honored stone and dormant greenery that seemed to spread out as far as one could see, "This," he repeated dramatically with a broad histrionic sweep of the arm, "must be the Kingdom of Heaven. I seem to have seen it all before, perhaps in my mother's womb." He laughed: "Could I guess, five minutes ago, how prophetically I spoke or how soon my promise of Paradise for you would be fulfilled? The prophet is perhaps, after all, not so much the man who foresees what must happen as the one whose promises are doomed to be fulfilled, in the same way as there was light as soon as God said: *'Let there be light.'*"

This interpretation of the prophetic gift disturbed me: "If you really are a prophet, Paul, you should be more careful of your words. Think of the responsibility for instance, of saying *'To Hell with you'* to some poor man and immediately consigning him to damnation for all time."

Paul shrugged his shoulders: "It's all the same, whichever way you look at it. The things that happen were all bound to happen anyhow. If the prophet is really a demiurge, he surely has enough divine wisdom to damn only those who deserve damnation. Whether determined by the prophet's words or merely foreshadowed in them, the event itself has the same moral value."

I was not convinced, but again hesitated to disagree, perhaps out of sheer intellectual laziness. We had now crossed the bridge and were walking across a lawn towards the first buildings of the city. "Well, here we are," Paul exclaimed joyfully, "in the New Jerusalem which is also old because eternal, world without end or beginning. And I'll buy you an ice-cream cone if we meet Tom here. It would be most inappropriate if the foolish pupil had been admitted to Paradise before his wiser master. Why, I would then have to write a stiff letter of complaint, in rhymed heroic couplets, to the Lord God of Sabaoth."

Paul was dressed, as usual, in clothes that scarcely suggested the master philosopher. His green baseball cap was set at a jaunty angle above his horn-rimmed glasses. He wore a blue-and-white sports shirt, striped horizontally, old and very dirty dark blue slacks, torn in the seat of the pants to reveal equally soiled underwear beneath, and very shabby sneakers, once white but now a dirty grey. All this would have suited a neighborhood urchin; but Paul always maintained that there is no official costume for philosophers and that only sophists assume a false

68

wisdom by wearing sombre clothes which, to the unwise, suggest a ponderous wisdom. The true philosopher, Paul would explain, is like Tiresias: one day man, the next day woman, the third day child. But Paul did not illustrate this theory consistently: we nearly always saw him dressed as a male urchin, rarely as a mature man, never as a matronly woman or a little girl. There was now something, which I pointed out to him, of the Yankee at the Court of King Arthur in his absurdly urchinlike figure as he ambled about the august vistas of the Kingdom of Heaven.

"Only your historical sense should be offended by my anachronistic appearance," he replied cheerfully. "I am at least in character: a figure from a twentieth-century pastoral of American industrial suburbia. In its details, my costume is not that of the tatterdemalions, shepherds or brigands, who traditionally grace such Piraneselike perspectives as these. But how was I to know that we would find ourselves here?"

Still, I felt that, at any moment, we might be arrested for trespassing. I began to wonder whether my own rather conventional dark and well-pressed suit was indeed more appropriate. This might, at any moment, turn out to be the most formal occasion of my life; and, for all I knew, my clothes might be as inappropriate as Paul's. I remembered having read, somewhere in the memoirs of a White Russian diplomat, that men must wear formal evening dress, tails and a white tie, for an audience with the Pope. But the Kingdom of Heaven is a Vatican City only by analogy; and audiences with the Pope are planned long ahead, whereas we had found ourselves here, as Paul had pointed out, most unexpectedly. I racked my brains but could remember, in all my readings, no precedent to suggest the proper costume and behavior for this unique occasion.

The first building we reached was a huge rectangular palace, perhaps an administrative building or a barracks. Its vast and severe façade was adorned only by long rows of windows. From the lawn, we entered an arcade; as we followed it to the left, we saw water. The building seemed to overlook a canal there, with steps leading down from another arcade to the water. A few brightly painted mooring-posts were cemented into the lower steps; beyond the canal, other buildings lined the canal or rose on three sides of a small plaza that overlooked it. Along the wall of the arcade, doors led into the building, some now open, others closed. The arcade was deserted when we entered it to the left, then turned. Through the first arch of the furthest arm of the arcade that we now left behind us, we could see more lawns. Approached from either of these two sides, the building was apparently the first of the whole city. So we turned to the left, towards the canal.

The first door that we passed was closed. Our steps, as we walked, echoed in the vaulted ceiling of the arcade. Between the few doors, huge expanses of empty wall stared blindly at us, stained with large spots where moisture had mimicked grotesque faces and fabulous beasts. Paul took out of his pocket an old stub of chalk, went up to the wall and began scrawling on it:

NUTS TO PEOPLE!

I suspected him of wanting to write something obscene, in the usual style of his toilet-wall remarks. But I was still shocked when this inscription turned out to be quite mild: "Paul, how can you behave like this? After all, we don't know where we are. Even if this is, as you say, the Kingdom of Heaven, you can see that nobody, in all the centuries of its existence, has yet had the nerve to scrawl inscriptions on its walls."

Paul laughed: "But this is only the paraphrase of a Biblical text, *Romans, 2:11*, 'There is no respect of persons with God.' Had I been a monumental mason, I might have inscribed the original text here in deep-cut gothic lettering, and you would not have objected. But my medium is chalk, so that I had to express the same lofty thought in more commonplace words."

As we argued, we walked ahead and reached an open door. I tiptoed up to it, peered in. Within I saw a huge library, all its walls lined with shelves full of old leather-bound volumes. Long tables, laden with astronomical instruments and all the paraphernalia of the classical chemist and physicist, furnished the centre of the room. At the nearest table, an angelic figure sat, dressed in brown monkish garb, deeply immersed in his reading. From the loose cowl, long golden locks fell over a face whose features were almost feminine. I beckoned to Paul, who seemed about to inscribe some other text on the cloister wall outside. Paul immediately joined me in the open doorway.

"Oh," he exclaimed, "*Non Anglus sed angelus*. This is a veritable houri, devised by some Old Man of the Mountains for the pleasures of the Elect. Come, boy," Paul added in a loud voice, half commanding and half cajoling, as he roused the angelic figure from its studies, "come and play with me!"

70

I retreated rapidly from the doorway into the arcade, ready to run away in sheer terror. But the studious figure looked up from the book, stared at Paul, smiled, rose from his seat and slowly came over towards the doorway where Paul was still standing. I watched them both as they stood there together, leaning against the door-post. The angel was still smiling, his body almost touching Paul's as he placed a hand on Paul's shoulder and allowed the loose sleeve of his monk's robe to slip back and reveal a dazzling bare arm that seemed sculptured in sheer light. I saw the lovely flesh flicker, like an old movie where the consecutive images jerkily imitate motion. But it was not change in position that made this arm of light flicker; the arm was actually changing its nature rapidly, appearing in turn as a lovely white and soft woman's arm, wearing two diamond bracelets, then again as a brawny, sun-tanned young man's arm, covered with a light down of glistening golden hairs, while the two bracelets swiftly became a blue tattooed eagle and the letters: U.S.N.

I watched Paul and the angel standing there in the doorway, both silently smiling. Suddenly, Paul seized the angel by the shoulders and they kissed. As they drew apart, the angel smiled coyly and exclaimed: "My! You kiss just like Renzo!" Paul seemed puzzled, but the angel took him by the arm, drew him into the library and closed the door. I too was puzzled, left alone in the arcade: man or woman, angel or demon, this creature was surely the first that could claim to have been kissed by both Paul and Renzo.

I paced the arcade nervously, back and forth past the closed door. All this was absurd. Paul could never be trusted. I now expected, at any moment, a painful scandal. We would be ejected from this odd Kingdom of Heaven ignominiously, without even the pathos of Adam and Eve driven forth from the Garden of Eden or the Miltonic grandeur of fallen angels. Ours would be, at best, the quick getaway of petty criminals fleeing the cops; or else, the arrest, *in flagrante delicto*, of undesirable trespassers who, after a brief stay in this Eternal City's county jail, would then be dismissed with a kick in the pants. I dared not imagine what our fate would be if it came to the worst. In my mind, I prepared long arguments of protest, ready for Paul's return. Should he not return, should this door never open again? I scarcely felt courageous enough to pursue alone my exploration of this city. I would wait here some twenty minutes and, should Paul fail to return within that time, then try to find my way

71

back across the lawns to the bridge. I waited, but soon discovered that I had no watch to keep count of the minutes as they went ponderously by. Whole ice-ages seemed to pass as I stood there, painfully frozen in fear and indecision. Should I go away alone? But how would I find my way home? At last, the door opened and Paul stood there smiling:

"Edouard, why don't you come and join us in the library? Antinous says he has a pal who speaks French and would enjoy meeting you. He'll be along in a couple of minutes."

I protested that I had no desire to take liberties which, I was sure, were condemned here even more strictly than on earth. Paul's answer cleared some of my intellectual doubts, but still left me emotionally disinclined:

"Surely, Edouard, the Lord God of Sabaoth is by definition omniscient. He must always have known all my virtues and vices; he probably even expects me to practice them here as on earth, now as heretofore. It would be foolish to invite a beggar to a rich feast and then object to his table manners. . . ."

I remained doubtful, though Paul indeed seemed delighted with his experience. He waited a while in silence, till his thoughts and mine were interrupted by a loud whistling in the distance, echoed everywhere around us in the vaulted arcade. Only Tom had this habit of whistling Bach's *Jesu, Joy of Man's Desiring* at all hours of day and night, always as loudly. I felt almost relieved as I explained to Paul that Tom must also be here, in this unorthodox Kingdom of Heaven; not only would this perhaps offer me the opportunity of bringing the episode of Antinous to a rapid close, but it might also mean that we, Paul and I, were not the only inappropriate intruders here, since I could scarcely imagine a less appropriate inmate for the Kingdon of Heaven, if that were truly where we were, than boisterous and indiscreet Tom. I suggested to Paul that we look for Tom. At the mention of his name, Antinous smiled:

"So you know Tom! He's often around here, and some of us find him rather fascinating, though he's always in a hurry and never seems to notice our existence or to know what he really wants. He just runs around wildly, always chasing after something that he never seems to find. And he's so clumsy too, all arms and legs and loud whistling. . . ."

Paul laughed. The whistling seemed to be coming towards us, now louder and clearer. Suddenly, as if Tom had turned away from us down some side-street, the tune began to grow fainter.

I told Paul that I thought we ought to go and look for Tom and find out from him, since he was apparently a frequent visitor here, a few facts about this place. But Paul was unwilling to leave Antinous; besides, he doubted whether Tom could give us any reliable information, since he always lives in a private world of his own which has very little relationship to the physical world in which he ceaselessly wanders. Who could ever trust Tom's description of any experience? Still, Paul suggested, if I wanted to look for Tom, why didn't I wander off and return in about an hour to meet him and Antinous? "If you find Tom, please don't bring him along with you," Paul added.

So I left Paul and his angel friend. They returned to their library, closing the door behind them. I began walking along the arcade towards the canal. Countless other doors, exactly like the one that led into the library, stood closed all along the inner wall of the arcade; I realized now that I had forgotten to count the doors, so that I no longer knew which one led into the library. Still, on my return, I could always wait here in the arcade until the right door opened and Paul would come out to look for me. But if he decided to wait inside, behind the closed door, until I, returning, opened it? I had not yet dispelled my doubts and fears when I reached the canal. There, I saw that the arcade continued, at a right angle, along the other side of the building. Beyond the canal, there were lawns leading to other buildings: a palace with odd bulbous domes, twisted columns framing its doors and windows, and Berninesque spiral towers at the four corners of its roof. Down each tower, stone balls rolled slowly, guided by some invisible mechanism that made them emerge, every few minutes, from a hole at the narrow tip of the spire, then roll slowly down the conical spiral path till they disappeared at the bottom, but so slowly that they seemed almost ready to stop or perhaps to start rolling upwards. I was fascinated and nauseated by their motion, so excruciatingly slow and hesitant, so very much like the motion of my own thoughts that I could barely detach my eyes from them, as if the motion of these balls, a perfect substitute, replaced for me the need for any thought. I stood there, watching the rolling balls from the brink of the canal, till I was awakened, so to speak, by the sudden return of Tom's whistling. He seemed to be quite close to me now, somewhere along the arcade that echoed his tune, still the same.

I resumed my search: there was nobody to be seen anywhere

73

in the arcade. I followed the deserted arcade, keeping the canal to my left and a blank wall, with no doors in it, to my right. When I had progressed some twenty yards, I found a small open door in the wall, so small that it was apparently concealed, in perspective, when I first looked down this arcade. Tom's whistling seemed to blow forth in violent gusts from this door. I entered, found a dark and narrow spiral staircase and began to ascend.

Endlessly, I climbed, lured ahead by Tom's whistling which, however, began soon to grow fainter, though I was going as fast as Tom usually went. The steps were damp and slimy. I fought my way upwards through age-old cobwebs that clung to my face and hands. The only light came from occasional narrow slits in the stone wall, like those from which, in ancient castles, the archers shot their arrows. Breathless from climbing what must have been hundreds of steps, I found myself at last at the top of the stairway, opposite a small open door that led into an organ loft vertiginously suspended above the deep nave of a deserted cathedral.

I looked down, beyond the loft, at the huge space ahead. Between the cathedral's pillars, torn tapestries fluttered in the gusts that blew through the broken stained-glass windows as shafts of raw light poured through the gaps left by missing pieces in their brightly-colored patterns. Heavy cobwebs spread all over the building, some so vast as to stretch from pillar to pillar or from side to side, clear across the chancel. Huge dead spiders hung motionless in some of these webs, as if crucified there. Beyond the choir, no candles or ornaments stood on the altar where the cloth was torn and stained beneath a tall broken crucifix that stood there askew, with one of its arms lopped off so that it looked more like a tottering gallows above the fallen and shattered figure of Christ that lay like a dismembered corpse on the altar steps. I was puzzled: had religion fallen upon such evil days that even here, in this ambiguous Kingdom of Heaven, its churches stood abandoned by the angelic choirs, slowly disintegrating in dust, ruin and oblivion?

My dismal meditations were interrupted by a sudden cascade of discordant notes, like those of an old mechnical piano, their wild mirth as joyless as the grotesque cackling of old women. Someone was playing the organ, laboriously picking out the notes of *"And they don't wear pants, In the Southern part of France. . . ."*

74

I entered the loft and discovered there our old friend Renzo. He was seated at the organ and, as he played his jerky little tune, kept turning to glance at the altar behind him, as if he expected something to happen there. Indeed, something did soon begin to happen.

As if attracted by the music of this Anti-Orpheus, two large bats suddenly appeared and began to circle wildly round the tottering crucifix. Then what must have been the sacristy door was opened stealthily and Antinous appeared. Renzo at once changed his tune to *"The flat-foot floogey with a floy-floy."* Shimmying wildly and gathering his monkish garb up to show his legs, the boy-girl stomped up the steps towards the choir and there broke, in front of the altar, into one of the wildest dances I have ever seen. Renzo seemed delighted and, as he continued playing his tune, punctuated it with enthusiastic cries: *"La mossa! La mossa!"*

After each one of these imperious cries, Antinous interrupted his antics for a while to perform a brief muscle-dance, then returned to the jazz rhythm of his disjointed shimmy.

Both Renzo and Antinous were soon exhausted. Renzo stopped playing and Antinous and the bats vanished immediately. Renzo then turned to me (he had noticed my presence, while still playing, and had winked at me knowingly each time that Antinous so obligingly danced *la mossa*) and exclaimed: "Isn't that nun the most wonderful dame you've ever seen? Gee, what a girl! Such hips (his hands drew generous curves in the air)! And such a smile (he blew a kiss, with the tip of his fingers, towards the deserted altar)! What a dame, what a dame!"

Suddenly, I understood why I was so unhappy here, in this Hell of a Kingdom of Heaven, so unsure of myself whereas others, Paul, Tom and Renzo, all seemed so secure and happy. Antinous and the other angels were all sexless: and that was why, to mere humans, they appeared as men or women, adopting in turn the form of each known object of human desire. *Nihil in intellectu quod non prius in sensu*: because angels can be perceived only intellectively, our perceptions of them must adopt the appearance of sensual perceptions already existing in the mind, already known and desired. Paul saw the angels as boys, Renzo as girls; Tom, desiring but himself, chased all over the Kingdon of Heaven after his own elusive self, never seeing anything, never wanting anything but this pursuit, always invisible (otherwise he might see himself) except to the angels.

And I, desiring nothing, saw the angels alternately as men and women, according to the appearances that I saw desire adopt in the minds of others.

I felt desperately lonely. I turned away from Renzo, ran out of the organ loft, down the endless spiral staircase, anxious to escape at any cost from this ghastly Paradise. Suddenly, I slipped and fell headlong, rolling down the steps till I lost consciousness, stunned by my sorrow and pain.

Chicago, 1939

PSYCHOLOGICAL NOVELETTE
WITH ONLY ONE THEME
AND PRACTICALLY ONE CHARACTER

*for Kurt Seligmann, who
illustrated these in VVV.*

1.

Early Childhood

Little Pamphilus Weathercock is seated on a high chair in the family kitchen, his legs dangling; still too short to reach the floor. He is weeping bitterly while he watches his mother, at the kitchen table nearby, slicing a long golden loaf with a big sharp knife. Each time she cuts a new slice, Pamphilus winces and bursts into a fresh spasm of sobs, then slowly calms down while she butters the slice soothingly with thick soft butter. And this is repeated several times, all very monotonously, without much variation except that, every once in a while, Pamphilus sees his mother eat one of the slices of buttered bread; and then, each time, his sobs reach a paroxysm so violent that he almost thinks he is about to die. And then his mother, who does not otherwise seem to be very much worried by his grief and pain, smilingly and with theatrical gesture of affected tenderness offers him a bite of the slice of this beautifully buttered bread of which she herself has just eaten. And each time he angrily refuses, almost vomiting at the mere idea of eating it.

2.

Puberty

Little Pamphilus Weathercock suddenly discovers that he is really much bigger than he had ever yet thought. But he is still, at the same time, as small as ever, if not smaller. In fact, there are two of him, the usual small Pamphilus now suddenly facing another new huge self, an enormous head, bearing all his own familiar features but grinning at him with a vast open mouth. Pamphilus easily recognizes himself in the huge features of the giant head whose hot breath smothers him. Inside the vast

mouth a large soft red tongue stirs, as if about to speak. But little
Pamphilus does not want to hear what big Pamphilus is about to
say; so, to prevent his giant from speaking, little Pamphilus
thrusts his two small arms into the huge mouth and firmly grasps
the tongue with both hands. It is slippery and hard to hold, but
little Pamphilus still manages to grasp it and begins to tug hard.
Slowly, he feels the huge slimy thing yield as he tears it from its
roots. With exquisite pain, little Pamphilus watches his own
huge face grow purple with agony, the glassy eyes popping out
of their enormous sockets, as he pulls harder and harder until he
swoons into daylight.

3.

First Courtship

Beneath the tall black sky, little Pamphilus stands, a small,
lone, luminous figure in the vast dark. Far above him, he
watches passionately something luminous and pink which
revolves high in the sky, hazy and beautiful like a blurred rose of
clouds. Little Pamphilus is desperate: the dreadful space
between him and his distant rose! Suddenly, with an agonized
gasp, he falls on his knees, on the hard black earth, and cries
out: "My God!" At once, there is a rumbling of thunder and the
rose, instead of being so small and far away, is huge and close to
his face, within his reach; and, instead of revolving, it now
stands suspended there, dreadfully still. Little Pamphilus then
discovers, to his horror, that it is no gentle soft-petalled rose, but
a huge hard and curled pink sea-shell, with sharp teeth all along
the two edges of its opening from which the hairy spidery legs of
a hideous hermit-crab protrude, slowly stirring in the night air
and reaching out greedily towards him. Little Pamphilus
screams and swoons, as usual.

4.

Choice

The top of the table was rolling with the regular motion of
waves, like the surface of the deep sea, beneath the rattling

78

white saucers. In each saucer, a large white cup, half full of black coffee which swirled in the cups as they were shaken by the regular motion of the table. Only occasionally, however, did any of the coffee spill over the edge of a cup into its white saucer. Most of the saucers were spotlessly clean, and there were well over a hundred cups there, each in its saucer, all of them half full of coffee and arranged in regular rows, five or six deep on the long table.

Little Pamphilus watched them dispassionately, though he knew that all these lovely cups were dancing there only for him to choose one of them, only one. But he also knew that he need not choose. They were there for him to choose only if he wanted to choose; and it was perhaps better not to choose. So he watched the rattling white cups for a long while, himself standing motionless while they moved. And motionless he watched them until some coffee had spilled into every saucer on the table. Then the table's motion became wilder, as if it were impotently angry at his refusal to choose a cup. Finally, one of the cups, with its saucer, fell off the edge of the table and broke at his feet. Then Pamphilus knew that, without having chosen, he was now married to this broken cup.

5.

Married Life

Pamphilus Weathercock is proud of his home, his income, his car, his well-fitted kitchen and his wife. So many things that he seems to control, to have created alone and almost out of void! He is reading his evening paper in the living-room when his wife calls him peevishly to the kitchen: "Do I have to do all the work? Come and open this can."

Dutifully, Pamphilus answers her call. She hands him the can, with bright yellow apricots on its label, and an ugly can-opener with a sharp and vicious-looking point to it. Dutifully too, Pamphilus strikes the top of the can with the opener, afraid at the same time that the point may slip on the smooth surface and, evading his control, cut his hand. But he pierces the can at once and, to his surprise, sees a drop of dark red juice trickle out instead of the yellow juice which he had expected. He continues cutting the can, then raises the loose lid. At first, he thinks he sees dark red plums floating in their juice. Then he suddenly recognizes the can's contents: a man's genitals, curiously like his own, soaking in thick red blood.

6.

Intimations of
Approaching Middle Age and Death

Pamphilus is walking along an immensely long and very luminous road which stretches out ahead of him, in the dark, as far as he can see, ever narrower as it speeds straight ahead to a point at the furthest imaginable horizon, without a curve, without a hill in its whole length ahead of him. Pamphilus sees that he still has very far to go through the dark along this dreary road; but he is depressed by its apparent narrowness rather than by its length as he looks down and notices that the road is only just broad enough, where he now stands, for him to walk along it. The road grows narrower and narrower ahead of him; then too, he notices for the first time that, above him and beneath him and to his right and to his left, everywhere else except along this road, there is nothing but a bottomless deep night.

Pamphilus wants to turn back. But he then discovers that, behind him, the road grows wider till it stops at the hilt of a huge sword along whose narrowing blade he has apprently been walking all this time. And from the hilt behind him to the place where he now stands, the whole blade is slippery with dark blood that drips noiselessly into the bottomless darkness below. Pamphilus steps forward, further along the blade and away from the blood. But the blood follows him like a rising tide and he suddenly realizes that, the further he walks along the blade, the further this blood, from his feet, will creep ahead, all the way from the hilt to the inevitable point, not so far away now, where the sword meets the horizon ahead. And no retreat is possible, back to the hilt along the gory blade.

New York, 1942

LETTERS FROM A LOST LATIN EMPIRE

for James Laughlin

I. *Nihil in intellectu quod non prius in sensu*

A threat of insects haunts my room. Time expresses itself in the woodwork as a discontinuous ticking, interrupted by frequent long pauses that correspond to my own forgetfulness when nothing seems to happen. But everything is always happening somewhere, whether I witness it or remain unaware of it, whether time pursues its ticking in my ears or seems to have relented for a while.

Across the ceiling a lone fly slowly crawls towards its death, its wings already numb and motionless from the cold of approaching winter. In a moment of prophetic memory, I consult the oracles of the past and think of all the things that have failed to happen, of all that I once planned to do but have never done. Behind me, the pages of my past diaries rustle like dry leaves as invisible hands finger through them. If I look out of my window at the broad and peaceful panorama of the future, I know that I'll see a landscape that I've never yet seen but that looks like all others that I've already known. Who can invent an entirely new kind of sky, an unprecedented sea-shore, preposterous hills and surprisingly novel trees? Where can I find a custom-made rock to suit only my own purposes and tastes?

Elsewhere, someone idly mentions my name in a quiet room, behind drawn curtains. He asks for news of me and wonders why I'm no longer reprinted in anthologies of living poets. Am I dead? Even I sometimes wonder if I'm still alive. For many years, my daily life has been but a long series of useless and frustrating jobs, filling with water baskets that leak, lecturing in empty halls to their echoing walls, emptying the ocean with a teaspoon into the bottomless pit: all this is interrupted only by hurried and tasteless meals or dreamless periods of sleep.

There was a time when I was still free to chase and collect butterflies. Now I scarcely ever see any in the fields. Have they, like my dreams, become extinct? Or is there no longer any real countryside, only an elaborate automated artifice as a substitute for nature? I can still remember natural colors, tastes and sounds that I no longer experience, words too that I no longer hear on anyone's lips. Daffodil? Yoyo? Astrolabe? Wimp? Sassafras? All my desires now strain towards the past, aroused by what is absent and can no longer happen, rather than towards anything that I'm still likely to experience here. I speak a dead latin that only I can understand.

II. *De profundis*

Condemned eternally to inspect my own stools like a curiously apprehensive cat, I lead a secret life of shame. The women have abandoned me, intent on evading all issues that are too terrestrial for their delicate sensibilities. They think they are angels, but I know better and they suspect me of it and hate me for it. Swathed in glossy textures of artificial fibres and redolent of synthetic essences, they wheel around me at a safe and decent distance, like ecstatic planets set in their revolving empyrean, always to the same perpetual canned music that mimicks that of the real spheres. Every once in a while, one of them will abandon her motionless and trancelike stance, when she reaches her zenith like an animated figure on an ancient clock as it strikes the hour, and she then insults me with a threatening and obscene gesture or a hideous grimace that contorts her angelic make-up into a devilishly grinning mask.

But I'm no longer sensitive to all their simian tricks. For all I care, they can pursue their present course in their chosen orbits until Doomsday. I'm content with my own little old Hell, with my own familiar degradation, with my pile of dung where I can crow like a cock, should I feel like greeting one of them when she rises above me as if she were a derisive sun that fails to bring me any light and warmth.

III. *Gloria in excelsis*

The Presidential residence is a veritable White House of crystal clouds, set in the midst of cerulean lawns of serene sky. A complex hierarchy of public relations experts and secretarial protonotaries, all jealous of their rank and privileges, keeps us regularly informed, through the mass media, of the various ceremonies which constitute the daily life of our intangible and august rulers whose absurd fantasies we are condemned to witness because we were once foolish enough to elect them.

82

Their breakfast, we're told, consists of duly desecrated Holy Wafers that are served to them by nude unfrocked priests on plastic dishes manufactured in a plant where the capital city's garbage is ingeniously recycled so as to produce this rare and precious material that can thus be put to new uses. After a timely fifteen-minute pause in the course of which our President, his family and his various personal assistants can retire to their fabulous toilets (they were revealed to us recently in all their splendor in a television broadcast which left us speechless with wonder), ambassadors and other foreign dignitaries or the Governors of our States are ceremoniously received in a hall lined with distorting mirrors where nobody can recognize even himself and nothing can possibly appear to be real. Credentials drafted in Tamasheq, Samoyede, Quechua, Frisian and other widely spoken languages are translated simultaneously over a public address system while the ambassadors read them softly into a microphone. This difficult task is carried out by a staff of highly trained presidential interpreters recruited from the aviaries of the Capital's Zoological Gardens. Each one of them, of course, must have previously obtained security clearance; for this, the color of the egg from which each was originally hatched is of primary importance. Recently, a subversive magpie, hatched from a carefully painted egg, was detected among them and proven to be a secret agent of the Soviet of Toads. It was tried, duly condemned, executed and roasted with garlic and a rice stuffing, then served as a grim warning to a prison inmate, for his Sunday dinner.

I could go on for a long while describing the fascinating byzantine ceremonies that distinguish the habitat of our splendid rulers in our distant capital. The higher ranks of the military, in particular, might well deserve special attention. Some of our colonels are said to have been able to obtain more rapid promotion because they were able to reveal a cloven foot. At General Staff meetings, some high-ranking officers strip to compare the lengths of their tails; in the paratrooper units in particular, prehensile tails can prove useful for displays of air-borne acrobatics. Others, whenever they appear on duty, make an impressive display of their virility, wearing enormous plastic cod-pieces beneath their uniforms and ingeniously contrived prosthetic arrangements of artificial hair on their wrists. At night, however, one can generally meet them as outrageously disguised transvestites in the cheaper brothels

83

frequented by drunken enlisted men. Such a double life is, of course, in perfect keeping with our democratic principles. Our Commanding General, for instance, is particularly popular with the troops and has every right to boast that he has already been almost every enlisted man's wife. Many an army wife is grateful to him for the pregnancies that she has thus been spared.

Much could also be written about our devoted secret police and our ideal fiscal administration. But why continue? A strong gust of fresh wind has just blown away all this imperial splendor like autumn leaves carried off in a destructive swirl or like scurrying clouds whose once magnificent shapes must merge and fade. Beneath a sky that's uniformly blue, we already live happily without any rulers.

Santa Cruz, California, 1971

SELECTIVE SERVICE

for Parker Tyler

After we had burned our draft-cards much as our forefathers had once emptied tea-chests into the sea, we expected at long last to be utterly free, though no two of us could yet agree on what to do with our hard-won freedom. The first few days were therefore devoted to parliamentary deliberations and passionate debates in the course of which rousing speeches were delivered, many of which quoted the authoritative but conflicting opinions of great thinkers of the past, the present and the future. A new order had to be instituted to replace the old, from which we had seceded. Decisions were taken on a mere show of hands, but each in turn was rejected as tyrannical by the minority which had just been outvoted. In an infinite regress, other new orders were soon approved, each one for a smaller seceding community.

Meanwhile the mills of the invisible gods continued to grind implacably. Selected by the silent machinery of death's inscrutable computers that are generally fed with dubious misinformation, every day one or two of us disappeared, some by accident in the increasingly unruly traffic of our congested roads, others from overdoses of self-inflicted artificial hells, others too as victims of the sporadic violence that followed each decision and the establishment of each new order. Statistics thus began to prove very soon that we were still subject to the same irrational fate as if we had retained our draft-cards. We had only chosen to avoid a soldier's death on the distant battle-fields of Samara, and instead to be victims of cancer, collision at cross-roads or what-have-you.

QUESTION PERIOD

Thanks to the miracles of modern medication, each day I now find my health improved, so that I'll soon be able to forget the dire warning of the incurable disease from the clutches of which I've momentarily escaped. As I now progress along the path that must nevertheless lead me inevitably to my ultimate death, I again feel free to formulate new plans for my future, almost as if I had truly become immortal.

Have I cheated death or has death cheated me? Is my health now a fraud? Is life a long chronic disease, with periods when it remains dormant and others that are rare crises, when the awakened bacteria become more virulent? How can one ever know what prophylactic precautions to take?

THE CONSPIRACY

I.

I often regret that my modest home lacks so many of the more modern conveniences and comforts, but I'm reluctant, after all these years, ever to face the trouble and uncertainties of a removal to other premises, if only because everything here is now familiar and can be trusted to age and deteriorate at my own speed. Anywhere else in this fickle, unstable and increasingly strange city, I find myself more and more at a loss to recognize my surroundings. A perpetual and protean frenzy of change afflicts them like some cancerous form of decay.

As soon as I open my door to go out on my daily errands, I already find myself on an utterly alien landing. Things have reached the point where I no longer even know how many flights of unfamiliar stairs I must descend before I reach the street, nor what street I'll find when I finally emerge on its sidewalk that I seem never to have seen before and that I'll certainly never see again. Conversely, when I've completed my errands in neighborhood stores where no salesman ever recognizes and greets me, I seem nevertheless to experience no difficulty in finding my way home! True, I may wander around for a while rather aimlessly, like a hound seeking a scent in the wilds. But I then need only to choose at random a street and a door, to climb any number of flights of stairs until I feel I've at last reached home. Before a door that I know I've never seen before, I stop without hesitation and can always fit my key into its lock. Beyond that door, I inevitably find my own familiar home, with all the books that I've accumulated through the years, all the dirty linen that I've failed to take to the laundry, the faded framed photographs of my dead parents and my lost loves hanging askew on the walls, my unanswered mail still lying on my dust-covered desk, my unwashed dishes piled up in the kitchen sink, all the objects of my distant and recent past that have become my regrets and forlorn hopes, reminders of my failings and failures. These are indeed my only true self. As soon as I see them, I recognize myself in them more readily than if I chance to see my own face reflected in a mirror that's nevertheless more faithful to my real appearance than the remembered image of myself that still haunts my laggard mind.

Though I choose my home each time at random in the city's puzzling maze of almost identical streets, somebody always seems to have known whither I was most likely to return from my errands. Whenever I open my door, I find messages awaiting me on the floor, slipped under the door while I was out. When I read them, I see that they are letters from unknown or forgotten friends, upbraiding me for failing to keep appointments with them, or from lawyers threatening me with legal action for failing to pay bills that I can no longer remember having received. But nobody ever rings my bell or knocks on my door when I'm at home, nor do I ever meet a single soul that I know when I'm wandering the crowded streets.

Are they really so crowded? How many citizens really inhabit this idle city that appears to be so busy, where all the streets are more or less alike and all the men and women wear the same expressionless mask, all dressed alike so that women can scarcely be distinguished from men? Only a few unschooled children sometimes look different, as if they hadn't yet learned the manners and ways of their more disciplined elders who then look at them disapprovingly.

We live in a peacefully ordered city, at the price of this deadly uniformity and anonymity. Often, I'm no longer quite sure of being myself, but I then recognize myself by the intimate disorder of my own thoughts and home, by my sense of failure rather than of achievement, by the vague memory, still haunting me fairly often though more and more faintly and infrequently, of having once lived elsewhere and differently, before something suddenly happened that I can no longer remember and may prefer to have forgotten.

II.

One day I woke up to the fact that I'm not alone to be alone. I began to recognize the symptoms of my own loneliness or lunacy in the faces and the behavior of others too. I even discovered that we, the lonely ones, constitute a secret élite in our otherwise democratically equalitarian city. We have our passwords, our almost inconspicuous signs and ways of greeting each other. We hold meetings now to which only the initiates are admitted. Should it ever become known abroad that we belong to this secret sect, we know that we have every reason to fear the worst.

But what can the worst be? Have we not already experienced, in this monstrously ordered world, the very depths of degradation? We invented our own hell when we voted the reforms on which we hoped to found our own heaven.

III.

We celebrate our unholy sabbaths in an artificial cave that manages to suggest to its inmates that they are well concealed from the unwelcome curious in the bowels of the earth or in submarine depths of the ocean. Nobody knows why we need the illusion of such womblike secrecy, nor would I be able to describe at all credibly the liturgy of our preposterous Masses. Anything I might say or write about them would immediately suggest that we must be insane to insist on such absurd precautions in concealing from the public eye such ludicrous ceremonies that anyone of sound mind would dismiss as commonplace or harmlessly infantile. Still, we have good reasons to distrust the suspicious authorities that rule us and, at the same time, we delight in our own secrecy and in our sense of doing something forbidden or subversive when we recite our pretentiously cryptic doxology in all seriousness, as if its meaningless obscurities were imbued with a magic too destructively powerful to lend itself to more public utterance.

Once a disloyal member of our fraternity was rash enough to divulge a part of our doxology to the uninitiate, who began to taunt us in public with our own secret phrases. Overnight, we were forced to change our whole ritual, after which some of our hymns, repeated to us by others in another context, soon failed to sound at all familiar in our ears. Instead of feeling that our old ritual was being profaned, we then began to dismiss it all as merely malevolent nonsense. Only in our own cave can our words sound at all meaningful. Only there can our otherwise commonplace ritual still purify us of our imaginary individual sins through participation in a greater collective sin that is sinful only because it is so secret.

IV.

In our neck of the woods, we've considerably improved on

89

nature by gradually eradicating the country's native flora. Instead of the usual trees, which all tend to grow in such an absurd variety of shapes, no two of them with the same number of branches, no two twigs with the same number of identical leaves, we now have man-made concrete tree-trunks, all exactly alike and all decked with the same number of identical branches, twigs and plastic leaves.

We're systematically improving on everything else too. To begin with, I even decided to improve myself and to live more reasonably. With this end in view, I chose a sensible girl and married her. In our new ideal home that is fitted with all the latest labor-saving devices, my wife often congratulates me and my fellow-citizens on our botanical and other initiatives. She no longer needs, for instance, to worry about dead leaves accumulating in the gutters of the roof so that the rain would no longer be able to flow freely into the drains.

We're also working on other and more vital improvements. My first-born still came into the world much as I and my wife had too, but my wife has recently been delivered of our younger child in a much more modern and hygienic manner: thanks to a pill that she had been taking regularly during her pregnancy, the infant came, after-birth and all, in a tidy disposable plastic bag. Unfortunately, the little angel was still-born, a martyr in the cause of progress, stifled in its air-tight container. We find consolation, however, in the knowledge that parents can still hope to improve the world for their children only by tenaciously trying out all new technological devices. Our scientists are still experimenting on mice with a new kind of pill that should be able to produce a bag of porous plastic around the foetus so as to allow it to breathe sufficiently while still avoiding the inconvenience of obsolete and less hygienic ways of coming into this almost perfect world.

V.

To the magic of the Evil Eye that is black, we oppose one that is blue, not white. For the Eye that is good is of the color of the sky and watches over us with a mother's protective love. We live beneath a protective dome of blue sky which shelters us from the evil that may well be hidden beyond its immeasurable vault, in those immensely distant regions where darkness and light are one and the same, where heat and cold are joined in the stillness of eternity.

A blue stone, a blue bead, is the sky's ambassador in our daily life. We wear it to protect us, day and night, against those evil forces of darkness and death, against the black magic of the Evil Eye that can turn you to stone, transmuting you into a statue or a corpse that will no longer breathe. On the white wall of your house, you may also paint a blue hand, to ward off the dark spirits of earth whose foul breath can breed disease in your hearth.

The blue Eye that watches over you reminds you too of your duties to self and to others. Its steady gaze is imperative, a mother's that guides and teaches you. Only from the Eye that is blue as the sky can you learn to be a man among men, no brute to yourself and to others. Remember the Eye that remembers you.

VI.

Who fails to see within a rose
Its glowing eye and in a wall
Its quivering lips can never learn
To live without the fear of death.

Paris, 1971

91

DIALOGUES AND MONOLOGUES OVERHEARD IN THE FIRE THAT REFINES

for Kenneth Rexroth

1.

—Apple or bomb, I tell you, it's no good.

—But it looks so juicy. . . .

—Sure it isn't a booby-trap? It might explode in your face.

—If it did, I'd never hear the end of it.

—Would you still have any ears to hear me tell you I'd warned you?

—Yes, when the Resurrection brings me back whole, foreskin and all.

—Does that mean that you'll then be a Gentile throughout all Eternity?

—Why not? Whether in Heaven or Hell, there's no longer much dividend in being one of Your chosen people and in always eating kosher.

—Has there been much dividend in it up till now?

—Now I know who You really are. You've given yourself away and shown me your cloven hoof.

—Are you a Pope to be still affirming that I've never ceased to exist? (Exit, farting sulfurously.)

2.

I was sure there could be nothing wrong in simply fooling around with the lovely little toy of flesh that I'd discovered at the bottom of my belly, between my legs. But they kept on telling me that my head would drop off my neck, some day when I would be grown up, if I continued to have this kind of fun with myself. Anyhow, all that happened many, many years ago, and I continued to play with myself, though always in secret and mostly alone in bed or in the toilet, and I still have a head on my neck, for all the good my head has ever done me. Maybe I would even have done better in life without a head, or crawling around without any legs in a kind of wooden box on wheels, or maybe my head might have continued living all by itself and without any body, always carried around on a silver platter like the

Baptist's head in those pictures of Salome. There's no knowing what might have happened to me if I'd chosen to be even more evil than I am.

3.

—She's a morphodyke.
—If she's that, why do you say *she*?
—Well, he's a morphodyke, if you'd rather have it that way.
—With those dragon-fly wings? I would've said it's an angel.
—With a tail sprouting out of its arse and that cloven hoof too?
—Where've you been all these years? Can't you see we're all like that? Only a saint can now tell whether we're angels or devils, and I've been dying for the past million years to find out what I really am. The trouble is there's been a scarcity of saints here ever since I've been around.

4.

My mirror never lies, but I'm really too devilishly beautiful even for a mirror. Others seem to see me only like themselves, covered from top to toe with slimy scales, but I know better, though I often hear others expressing, for their hideous selves, the same kind of admiration as I feel for myself. Can it be that each one of us is beautiful only in his own eyes and in his own mirror?

5.

—How many times, love, have I told you not to piss on the flower-beds?
—But I like to see the flowers shrivel up and die. It's nearly as much fun as pulling the legs off grass-hoppers.
—Some day, a big black devil might come along and piss on you too, my little flower.
—If I don't grab him first by his ugly pisser and pull it off his belly. . . .
—You naughty little girl! Where on earth do you learn such horrid thoughts and words?
—From listening to you and Dad having your fun.

6.

It was a beautiful summer day, without a cloud in the blue sky, with birds singing in the rich foliage of the trees and countless wild flowers scattered throughout the meadows that a gentle breeze ruffled like watered silk on which a host of angels might have been busy embroidering a many-colored pattern. Was I in Heaven? I could scarcely believe my eyes when, out of a a nearby cave at the foot of the hill-side, the scaly Monster, a kind of giant worm, crawled towards me, breathing fire from its hideously gory mouth and huge nostrils and roaring at me, from the depths of its infernal lungs, that it wanted a virgin served up immediately for its breakfast.

"A virgin," I gasped in dismay, "surely you mean a new-born babe. Where do you expect me to find you an adult virgin in this depraved day and age, unless you can be satisfied with a Lesbian?"

At that, the furious Monster tried to swallow its own thick and slimy tail, but only managed to choke and to scorch its arse-hole with its flaming breath, so that it died there in agony while I watched it writhe and squirm in a cloud of stinking smoke. Ever since that day, I've been wondering whether I'm a saint or a hero, Bellerophon or Saint George, but nobody believes me when I tell of my strange adventure.

7.

—Do it yourself. . .
—For love of self. . .
—All by yourself. . .
—Only for self. . .
—I for me. . .
—You mean an eye for an eye. . .

Paris, 1973

94

New Hieroglyphic Tales
(1929-1968)

FOREWORD TO
THE 1968 KAYAK PRESS EDITION

Habent sua fata libelli: in the Preface to his own *Hieroglyphic Tales*, Horace Walpole declared that they had been composed "a little before the creation of the world" and had ever since been preserved "by oral tradition, in the mountains of Crampocraggiri, an uninhabited isle not yet discovered," by clergymen not yet born. Walpole wrote his tales "about things that never were nor shall be," but that might yet be possible. He then printed and published only seven copies of them on his own private press at Strawberry Hill. Written "extempore and without plan," they were then reprinted in 1926, in an edition that is already rare. Wilmarth Sheldon Lewis, one of the few scholars who has ever deigned write about them, concludes his brief discussion of these little masterpieces of premature Surrealism as follows: "Although the twenty-fifth century may find the *Tales* commonplace, they are too extravagant for us. It is a struggle to accept a pistachio-nut drawn by an elephant and a ladybird, but a princess who speaks French in perfection and never was born is too much for us."

My own *New Hieroglyphic Tales* were likewise too much for the first publishers to whom I began to submit some of them in 1929, when I was nineteen. Written at various times between 1928 and 1966, most of these prose-poems have never been published until now. A few of the earliest ones were indeed published in *transition*, *Blues* and *Oxford Poetry 1929*. Others, later, in *VVV* and in an anthology of prose poetry that Charles Henri Ford edited for a New Directions Annual; then some of the earlier ones were reprinted by Vanguard Press in an anthology of work originally published in *transition*. When Louis MacNeice and Stephen Spender edited *Oxford Poetry 1929*, in which *Hand* was first published, I explained in a footnote that it was "a vision mantra," thus anticipating Allen Ginsberg's use of this term by a good quarter of a century.

Unborn clergymen somehow failed to preserve for me the manuscripts of my earlier prose-poems that remained unpublished. Suddenly, I found them again, however, in New York, in a trunk I had left there twenty years earlier, together with a grey derby hat and other improbable objects that survived the hazards of my wandering life. Meanwhile, another

97

miracle had occurred: a few years ago, Dutch friends suddenly mailed me clippings of an editorial published in Holland's leading literary weekly, *Elsevier*. A curious Dutch journalist had stumbled on an old copy of *transition* and found there my *Americans of the Future*, which he translated into Dutch, commenting on the prophetic quality of the "unknown" poet who, over thirty years earlier, had been vouchsafed this strangely correct vision of things to come.

All this has encouraged my to collect these poems now for publication. At most, I have corrected a word here and there, but not rewritten any of them. It feels good, at the age of fifty-seven, to make one's bow again to one's public, if one has any, in the guise of an eighteen-year-old poet.

Edouard Roditi
San Francisco, January 1967

MYTHS & MARVELS

(1)

Metamorphosis

There were no more faces.

One day above the western gate of the city there appeared a grey cloud shaped like a hand. As the hand came nearer it was seen to hold a glove; and when the hand was above the city like a dark sun at its noon, the glove fell.

Immediately all faces disappeared. A man who was buying an umbrella first became aware of this; he raised his head and saw that the salesman's face had been replaced by a large oval green leaf. He looked at his own face in a mirror and saw that it had also been replaced by a large oval green leaf.

The alarm was given. Men ceased to disagree over this or that. The goldfish in the bowl in Mrs. X's drawing-room ceased to think that they were the centre of the universe. All machines stopped and several dogs and cats were seen to fall down dead in the streets. Then the clock on the cathedral tower began to turn backwards. Stocks fell on the market and there was a general panic when people noticed that all the tickers and the radios were silent.

Ever since that day we have all been vegetarians; but it is forbidden by law to eat the large oval green bay-leaf.

(2)

Britannia Rules the Waves

On the island the fluttering gulls laugh when the statue rises with the sun and glides across the sea towards the west. The sea-weed coils its snakes around the statue's feet; the stars weep into the sea and their silver tears fade among the waves like fins of light.

No ship . . . the skeletons of waves devour each other . . . no ship to break the monotony of waves.

A small wave deposits a dead rat on the shore of the island where the restless gulls laugh. The statue immediately sinks into

the waves as if it had anxiously been awaiting this signal.
Laughing gulls, observe the importance of the dead rat!

(3)

Simultaneously

On the promontory, beside the fisherman's hut, stands the palace of light, sentinel warding off the advancing armies of waves. The lights of its windows are reflected far out across the sea to where the negro lies dying on his raft.

The negro dreams of a red flower and of palms on a distant shore, of departure and of shipwreck among flames and crackling planks.

The wily waves advance, bearing the raft towards the palace. When the raft reaches the rocks of the promontory the negro dies and the palace falls headlong into the waves.

The negro's soul rises, a red flower sprung from among the rocks, and is caught in the brilliant net of the stars. The fisherman returns to his hut with a red star-fish in his net.

(4)

Lunaire

At night faces appear in the chalices of flowers as they open to gaze at the moon.

There is a black poppy which gives birth to a head, a hand and a foot. The poppy's stem sinks into the earth where its roots cling to a curious carved stone. On the stone is a fish, symbol of lost love.

When the stone is unearthed the poppy will be forgotten. But if the stone is unearthed at night, the head, the hand, and the foot will also be found to be carved there and the fish will have faded away.

Seventy-Seventh Advent

When the steel axe fell into deep waters the trees shivered and the birds ceased to sing.

For many years the steel axe awaited its resurrection. Until one day, as a stranger passed along the banks of the river, all the lost coins and rusty nails rose from their muddy shrouds beneath the waters and imprinted their stigmata on the five-pointed stars of his hands. Last of all the steel axe flew upward with such force gathered from the struggles of its liberation that it lopped off the stranger's hand, which fell into the deep waters.

Now, among the silent birds, there is a rumor of a new resurrection promised to the hand, and of a steel stranger.

(6)

Séance

The stranger walks into the dark room where two men sit at the table and talk of travel. The stranger joins in the conversation saying: "I too have travelled"; and the two men look up and seem surprised at his sudden appearance. In the corner of the ceiling there is a sound of very swift wings, or of a muttering of motors and a chattering of thin voices. The stranger disappears. His voice is heard first in this corner, then in that, until it finally fades away somewhere near the small open window. Where the stranger stood the two men find a railway-ticket to an unknown destination.

(7)

Spiritual

On the vast terrace the white-robed beings stand and watch the flickering lights of cities which, far beneath them, shine through the thick waters of night. The fish-cloud swims slowly through the ocean of space, and the cities are obliterated by its shadow.

The white-robed beings see no more lights beneath them and

look upwards.

High up on the terrace there is a new understanding of the surrounding oceans of space and of the submerged lights. For, just as the white-robed beings have always known that invisible threads of light bind the unknown creatures scattered in the cities to the five-pointed stars of their own hands, so, looking upward, have they seen, springing from their own heads, other threads of light which all converge towards one extremely distant point where darkness and light are united in a perfect black diamond.

(8)

Old Wives' Tale

The network of twigs is etched against the background of the dying day. In the dark undergrowth, the invisible beasts of night are stirring the leaves and a warm moist breath attacks the hand with sudden fear of hidden teeth.

On the cold road, the rising moon shouts: "Ice." Not so long ago, the moon was red, or rather the damp summer had called forth an eczema of rust on the moon's pale steel face. But tonight the pale moon shouts "Ice" on the ice-white road which sleeps and dreams of legless and bodiless feet that run at random and forget their birth in pairs.

Feet and eyes and ears and legs and hands and arms are born in pairs. But the night tolerates the birth of single limbs and organs and its bushes are full of one-eyed beasts—have they a head, a body?—; then there are lonely ears listening in the flowers, and one eye watches you sometimes from between their petals.

Do not touch flowers at night. Do not speak to flowers at night. Do not walk abroad at night; but sleep and forget the dangers of night.

(9)

Aurora Borealis

A crystallization of color spreads from the upper regions of the dark sky towards the tremulous nipples of the waves. The feathery fringes of clouds fade behind pillars of green light. Transparent curtains tremble everywhere. In the arctic temple, the hidden Samson of light shakes the moon-green pillars of the night.

Color these crystals with sudden blood; it is dawn, or else the last consumptive saliva of the dying day. Heartless hard light!

In the crisp light of the frozen tinkling stars, no waters flow. The ice-stars are icebergs in this black ocean. When the green glass cathedrals crash, the light and the pillars of light and the green pillars of moon-green crystallized light are reflected through space and finally settle like sharp blades above the tremulous nipples of the waves.

Samson moves in the glass cathedrals. Samson and the bull and Samson and the sun and the sun is the bull and Samson is the sun and is the bull.

Let crackling twigs of green-white light weave fantastic tree-patterns on the mirror of the sea. Let the deceptive sky celebrate the fall of its ice-cathedrals and its icebergs and its ice-stars when darkness hardens the black waters into the sullen black ice-pack of night.

Red Samson the arctic red sun is moving in the groves of green pillars. There is the red tinge of consumptive blood flickering behind the moon-green glass pillars of light. Blood of red Samson, red blood of Samson, the red thief is sprinkling blood on the slanting pillars of the falling sanctuary of light that is doomed to succumb soon to the black ice-pack of night. Then there will be night and, suddenly thrust into dark night, the red sex of the Samson-sun must later rise out of eastern whiteness and destroy the night.

Then the pillars of the black shattered temple of night glow with a white light and a red light of consumptive blood, but again later comes night and again the same Samson as the temples crash each time that the red thief scatters blood on the pillars of the light or the pillars of the night. And the thief is Samson and the red sun is Samson and Samson is the thief and Samson is the sun.

(10)

The Infinite Cage

A cry in the night breaks a dark glass. Broken blades of mirror fall around the steel-edged voice, reflecting in their scattered swords disconnected fragments of mist-obscured dreams.

A tall obelisk alone is left vibrating whitely in the moonlight against a background of sound-absorbing trees that stir faintly in a dark and porous wind.

A cold clamor in the pierced sky. The steel shield of the moon is cast headlong into a black plashing pool. The earth sways on its foundations. Vertiginous lights flutter and spin across the pool. Then everything subsides into prehistoric quiet.

Through this timeless quiet, surrounded by shifting symbols, we must walk. Our feet leave no tracks on the soft soil. Images and symbols surround us, moving with a slow, implacable but irregular rotation. There are no shocks; only sudden fadings and superimpositions. Beyond these symbols, we can see nothing but squelching quicksands of thick darkness spread around and beyond us like the trackless soil on which we walk. Nothing can be changed. We leave no mark. To shout . . . but our throats are soundless, and there have already been so many shouts, so many shouts which have shaken the small sphere of sensual perception which surrounds us and where we walk, so many shouts have already scattered the shifting symbols and then everything has subsided again into this prehistoric quiet. To shout . . . and there is no use in shouting. It is better to keep quiet within this small surrounding sphere and to walk ahead, always surrounded by the world of our sensual perceptions, never any larger, never any smaller. As we walk, we are always haunted by the same shifting symbols, so that there is no progress and no change.

(11)

Greek Tragedy *

We follow the red rocks of a Grecian coast. Our sailingship

* Like other poems, this one is based on an actual dream in which the word cest was pronounced, like a pun on both incest and the word used in antiquity for the girdles worn by victorious boxers.

stands out, white and red, against the blue sea and sky. The guide points out the places of interest: lofty ruins and, beneath them, the caves now transformed into giant aquariums lighted from within. As we approach the promontory which juts ahead of us towards the horizon, we see a cave far greater than any of the others. Two streaks of vivid white light battle furiously and amorously within its luminous waters. "They are fighting in the royal cave!" shouts the panic-stricken guide into his megaphone. "Who can stop them?"

Next to the cave, a young man leans against a red rock and weeps. His tears are dissolving the rock and will soon have washed away the wall of the cave. At the precise moment when we land in order to prevent all these catastrophes, the glass aquarium-front breaks and torrents of brilliant seawater leap out of the cave. The cave is empty. *"Ils sont perdus,"* the guide mourns; he weeps as he blows his nose vigorously in a dirty red-and-white bandana handkerchief into which his black moustache has somehow become interwoven.

But in the foul depths of the dark cave one can still hear the sound of blows. Drops of blood splash out of the cave onto our clothes. "They have broken their *cests* on the brutal dark rocks," the guide remarks as he follows this tragedy intently from a safe distance.

Suddenly, from the depths of the cave, the incestuous twin athletes step forth. They are of an extremely luminous beauty, golden-haired and naked, with blood pouring from their fists and from between their legs. A door opens silently in the side of the cave and the athletes lead us into the royal apartments where our memories of this tragedy are soon wiped out by a swift return to the physical.

(12)

The Houses of the Dead

Sur les maisons des morts mon ombre passe
Qui m'apprivoise à son frêle mouvoir."
Paul Valéry

A moving shadow betrays death. The soft moon weeps upon white walls where a sudden shadow breathes new life.

105

Trees grow weary of silence and the moon slowly withdraws
behind clouds. When the moon appears again the glass of silence
is broken into innumerable lost fragments. Unknown feet weave
circles in the grass.

It is never too late for the death of death.

(13)

Virgin

I know that I shall never find in the darkness the only flower
that can ease her pain. Even by daylight the flower is concealed
in the grass. And now, unless some shooting star, attracted by
the magic virtues of the herb, falls on the small white flower, I
shall never find it.

Her joy or her pain depend on the erratic movements of a
star: frail chains of chance in a vast spider-web where fixed stars
are but dew-drops—in a web which can be torn by the fall of
one stray star.

The web remains unbroken, and I shall never find the magic
flower.

(14)

Hand

Clouds darken the plain.

From all sides, the mountains of the horizon move forward;
the plain shrinks, crumpled into valleys that grow deeper. The
three rivers become torrents that flow swiftly in their cavernous
beds towards those dark spots where they meet: the cities.

Then the sun again.

The mountains move back to the distant circular horizon; the
valleys disappear, and the three rivers flow placidly in their
scarcely perceptible beds of luminous sand. The cities glisten
with their crystal walls and the hard light is reflected from house
to house along the glass streets. Men no longer drag their
dark-blue shadows like long chains that rattled on the opaque
cobble stones. Silence of light: frozen wines of sound. No wind
stirs, sleepily coiled around the towers that are transparent stems

bearing the white flowers of clouds which float, vehicles for our pure thoughts, like water-lilies on the surface of a stream until they fade into the blue depth of space.

(15)

The Order of Things

On the right is a mound which sends forth a green jet of foliage. Beneath its shade, the Oriental Eve reassembles her scattered curves and listens to the bowed shepherd's pipes.

On the left and beyond these minor pastorals, there stands a city where the arcs of stone radiating from a central palace leap across the isolating waters of its moats.

And above and around these scenes the garish jewels of mechanical birdsong glitter on the neck of the sky, now complicated in the distance by an intricate design of banners (o virility!), of masts and of minarets.

Through a crack in reality's tortoise-dome, we can witness Indian pastorals and, in the distance, the sudden flowering of astonishing civilizations.

(16)

Fragment of a Novel about Lost Love

In this upper-moon beyond the loneliness of other moons, clouds drift slowly, dragging across the ground a long dark shadow, which has the perfect outline of your body. As I walk along the grey sands, following your fleeting dark-grey body, I feel the sands dragging me backwards while your shadow-body advances faster and faster; I run, but the gap between me and your shadow-body widens and widens until it is no longer a stretch of empty sands but a gaping precipice. Into this precipice I fall and find it full of dry rotting string and of cobwebs and dusty bones and ashes and dry leaf-mould.

Above me the stars shine and weep for the widowed moon who has lost the warmth of her husband's body and has grown so cold that now she no longer even feels or knows her own loneliness.

107

As I fall into the precipice I lose sight of the moon and of the stars and life is completely dead and death has completely fled.

I am left hanging in an uncertain void which is no longer void because nothing can rise nor fall nor move in it, but everything remains fixed and loses its very existence, so that I am left dangling in this nothing and wait for the small light of life which is no longer you.

And I know that you can no longer return because there is this precipice between us and I am left dangling in it but I know that another light must sooner or later come in your stead.

MIRAGES

(1)

The mystical masturbator performs his acts on a receding set of three empty and superimposed stages. On the lowest foreground, nearest the audience and almost within its grasp, he is grotesque, lewd, a clown. On the highest stage, where his actions cannot so easily be perceived by the audience, he is sublime, a spiralling dancer. There he is also surrounded by a blinding white light and by rhythms of pain. Between these two extremes, he is more often seen on a complex stage where his clever and artistic actions can please a more sophisticated audience. Here, modern, artificial, he probes his inner consciousness and, eloquently dull, delights his audience with a show of intellectualism and deep thought.

His actions on the first and the third stage are most easily understood by the masses. On the third, however, the lighting effects and the distance which separates him from the audience still make it difficult to follow all the mime's actions. The second and central stage, devoted to art, culture, and the subtleties of the day, is said to provide great intellectual pleasure to the elite, but is only a byproduct of this whole human tragedy.

(2)

In the palace of art, surrounded by all luxuries (deceit of hidden machinery, of silken surfaces and façades!) the corseted faceless creatures dance. The music is a quintessence of all that is useless, divorced from its fountainheads of love and religion. The women can easily be recognized, being of a finer texture and, on the whole, a *de luxe* article. The men, built for the hardships of sport, business and politeness, are of a home-spun quality (home-made in our own factories), and far more serviceable. There are also flowers and palmtrees grown in the heat of electric suns, very refined drinks (ah! fruits of chemical trees, synthetic Nature's factories!) that bear no trace of an earthy origin.

The music hopes to continue forever; in order to preserve this entertainment from death and decay (now obsolete), a large staff of clerks and scientists supplies the guests with passports for immortality and eternal youth.

(3)

The city of the Americans of the Future brandishes in the sky its phallic ten-thousand-floored buildings. The lower thousand floors are occupied by the inferior races of animals and men and by other such machinery. In the remaining floors above, the Americans of the Future live, distributed from top to bottom according to their wealth and business capacity. Between the buildings radiates an intricate network of bridges so that, when passing from building to building, the proud inhabitants of this city never need to tread the vulgar earth.

The Americans of the Future thus live in mid-air, at different distances from the earth—distances which vary according to the wealth of these highly-civilized men. Served by skillful contrivances, they no longer need any contact with the earth except for the healthful purposes of sport and travel. The earth is despised as a rather disgusting relic of past barbarism. All food is compact, chemical, and absorbed secretly in private or public conveniences. The generative organs of this race are male will-power and female acceptance of this will-power.

Living on such altitudes of the mind, they have forgotten their bodies and use them only automatically and unconsciously in the natural acts of life such as the bringing in and letting out of money which, for them, has replaced the more vulgar and old-fashioned usages of breath. They have also forgotten their souls, which have been entrusted to the devils of comfort, wealth, and efficiency and subsist only in an entirely dead and mummified form. The more abstract limbs of their minds are also slowly becoming atrophied and dropping off them like the useless legs of certain prehistoric lizards.

The Americans of the Future have amassed vast fortunes, which they call felicity; they have restricted life and the acts of life to a bare minimum, which they call progress; and they have suppressed all prehistoric faults and foibles that might deter or distract from the pursuit of a "disinterested" ideal which they call efficiency. The Americans of the Future die by accident, having suppressed by scientific means all forms of natural death.

110

But the race of the Americans of the future may some day become extinct; the earth will then remain to remind all future races that the Americans of the Future were astonishingly civilized, if one considers the early date of their empire and civilization.

DESCRIPTION OF THE LAST WOMAN

Her hair was the last gust of a torrid wind. Her eyes were the last moment of a suicide. Her mouth was the ultimate ocean. Her hands: the last idols. Her feet: the last foundations. Her body: the last temple.

One day she awoke beneath an iron tree: the last solitary awakening. One day she awoke in a garden and found no companions. One day she awoke and wandered among the steel flowers of a mechanical Eden; one day she wandered in the garden waiting for the night but the night never came. There was dawn. There was morning. There was even noon. And at noon all the wheels of the mechanical Eden whirred and chimed. But after noon the sun instead of sinking seemed to recede further and further into space.

(Her nails: the last tools. Her teeth: the last mill.)

And space and the sky were no longer blue and there were no more clouds; but space and the sky became an opaquely translucent greenish-grey fluid and the sun grew smaller and smaller until it reached the size of a small and poisonous-looking berry. Then the last woman noticed that the poisonous-looking sun was green and she lay down on the thin steel grass (how soft!) and wept. And slept: the last vision.

At first she only saw the steel flowers revolving and whirring as usual, and the steel birds flying backwards and forth on their accustomed steel tracks. But the birds passed back and forth more often and the flowers revolved more swiftly and the speed of everything seemed doubled. Then she noticed two bright green eyes which blazed behind a clump of mechanical rose-bushes; and the mechanical rose-bushes became red-hot and melted in this electric gaze. And thus, set in a face of shapeless iron vapor, the green eyes moved forward and destroyed another clump of trees; and advanced throughout the garden until the whole of the mechanical Eden had melted in their gaze. Now the paths of the metallic Eden were streams of molten steel teeming with vague forms of serpents, eyes, stars, fish, clouds, which disappeared into the molten mass and reappeared as birds, faces, hands, ships and breasts, which also disappeared and reappeared as button-hooks, umbrellas, syphons, chains, electric bells, which disappeared and reappeared as spirals, triangles, cubes, circles, and sinuous lines whose shape was never fixed but always changed until these also disappeared and left nothing but the swirling streams of molten steel. And when the whole of the last Eden was but one stream of molten metal, the green eyes wandered into the outer world.

(Her eyes: the last moments of a suicide.)

The last woman fled from the green eyes, ever feeling their burning gaze projected on her metal buttocks; and wherever she passed the green eyes followed her so that the whole world melted swiftly in their gaze. Cities burst into flames, crumbled into cinders, then joined the molten flood. Bridges collapsed and were dissolved in the streams of lava which flowed beneath the arches of the sky. Colonnades curled upwards like burning paper and rose in spirals to the sky, then fell to the ground in a heap of shapeless ashes. But there were no corpses.

(Her body: the last temple.)

And out of the city again the green eyes followed her into the swiftly-melting countryside. The last steel animals flared up in wild explosions then crumbled into ashes. The last trees sizzled, smoked, and were charred. Ashes. The hills melted, the rivers evaporated and their beds became torrents of molten matter; rocks were split by the heat, then melted into pools of white-hot glass; and death hovered in the sky in the form of one last small grey cloud.

Through the countryside the green eyes followed her to the bitter sea-shore. Here the sands became red-hot, then white, and melted. The burning sea-weed squirmed like snakes in their death-agony; and the white-hot sea-shells glittered like timid eyes scattered along the shore.

But the sea did not evaporate. For when the green eyes reached the sea, slowly the sea coagulated into one huge black slab of stone, the only solid left upon the whole earth, a black marble tomb for the sad fish that died there like flies caught in an opaque black amber. And in the cool silken depths the sea-weed ceased to flow and wave like the mystical hair of nymphs, the sea-weed now doomed to become immovable veins in an eternal slab of black marble. And the solidified sea ceased to live.

Still followed by the two green eyes, the last woman ran, breathless with fear, across the stone slab of the sea which spread out its endless black surface monotonously around her as far as the rim of the circular horizon; until suddenly, out of the molten lava of the continents, and out of the solid tomb-stone of the sea, rose clouds of small white petals, all petals of one vast flower

113

which formed itself slowly in the silent air, rising upwards and fading in the opaque green silence of space.

Then the last woman turned and faced the green eyes of the invisible angry face.

(Her eyes: the last moments of a suicide.)

And she gazed into the green eyes, her own eyes, and lay down on the black slab of the sea. And as the last woman's steel body stiffened, brittle relic exposed upon the black marble altar of a dead planet, out of her mouth rose a star: the last star.

THE PATHOS OF HISTORY

I.

On the stereoscopic screen that's here and now, the beams of past and future meet and enjoy a transitory reality. If you close your eyes, if you sleep or forget for a while to watch, if you but faint or fail to remember yesterday or to anticipate tomorrow, then nothing is real any longer, at least until you again give the show your undivided attention. The past is real as long as you see it now as a ruin, a setting for the present; the future, real only as the seed that you hold now in your hand, the seed destined to be a whole wheat-field in another time and another place.

Our mail is delivered to us each day from the past and we send our replies into the future. Each one of us lives in a different present that draws differently on yesterday and tomorrow. Only rarely do two or more of us experience simultaneously the same present, the same mixture here and now of there and then.

II.

A letter dated of the Year of the Colorless Death that has not yet befallen us came today to remind me of the pathos of the future. It spoke of our present as of a distant past that had come and gone mysteriously, leaving but monumental relics which already puzzled generations of archaeologists and curious tourists.

My correspondent, in his flight from the metropolitan centres where the great epidemic still raged, had sought refuge in a deserted area of ruins that stood in the midst of undistinguishable rubble. History-books, he writes, taught him something about our legendary wars, our bombings of our own cities, our "scorched earth" retreats. But what he now saw bore no trace of any greater violence than that of mere time and neglect, which destroy as thoroughly, though more slowly and less surprisingly, as any catastrophe contrived by man.

With a lyrical enthusiasm that was reminiscent at times of the best pages of Volnay or of Baedecker, he described to me the future ruins of our law-courts, of our Main Post Office and of the department store where I have a charge-account, sole

115

recognizable survivors of the architectural labyrinth that we daily tread in our search for tomorrow's spending-money. In a wilderness of rubble barely concealed beneath mounds of accumulated refuse where the weeds of centuries blossomed and withered, the towering vestiges of these three institutions still stood before his eyes, symbols of the culture of our age.

I feel that I must answer his curious missive promptly, while I can still describe a past that is no longer at all accessible to him, a present that already hovers, in his memory, on the misty brink of oblivion. Fortunately, he and I have our despair in common, our sense of doom: we speak a common language, the speech of those subversive elements that are accustomed to loneliness in a crowd and that see death and destruction where most of their contemporaries, more loyal or more sanguine, obediently dream only of amusement and profit.

III.

". . . Most poignant of all, an abandoned church on a hill above the sleepy harbor. A creaking wooden door hung loosely on a rusty, broken hinge. In the spacious dome from which the peeling plaster still fell like fine snow whenever a strong wind blew through the paneless windows, thousands of doves had nested. Their parliamentary session of alarmed cooings passed a vote of censure on my trespassing. The floor of the church was soft with their droppings and with the feathers of previous generations that had moulted there. The brittle bones of their dead lay buried in this accumulation of their own excrement and cast-off finery. . .

". . . In an open space among rotting wooden shacks where cheese-pale hags watched the street fearfully from behind their cracked and filthy window-panes, a drunken invader from the truck-farming suburbs slowly dismounted from his donkey, muttering threats that seemed to be addressed to his absent wife. He already knew that he would bring her but a meagre share of their week's earnings; he had been tempted to spend too much on drink on his way home from the market where he had sold, that morning, their crop of melons. Fumblingly, he tied the donkey to a dead fig-tree, unbuttoned his torn pants, addressed a ribald remark to his own swollen penis and then solemnly pissed against the desecrated sarcophagus of a forgotten prince

116

that stood on the sidewalk, tilted on its side, as if it had only just been tossed off a runaway hearse. . .

". . . Wide or narrow as my desire, the street leads through several centuries of the unrecorded personal history of long-forgotten nonentities, from the corner where I live, opposite the abandoned cemetery, to the next corner where passengers alight at the bus-stop and hurry away on business that cannot possibly bring them to my door. . .

". . . My day begins when a Muezzin's call summons me from my bed to watch the chilly grey dawn. Roused from a dream of gigantic cannibalistic women who cautiously conceal their quivering lips behind heavy veils, I leap to the window, stark naked. On his balcony across the street, the Muezzin is surprised to see me so unashamed; modestly, he looks the other way, down into the dark street. Together, we watch the cats slink among the refuse of the alley that separates my hotel from the mosque. In the flop-house across the street from my window, a half-naked stevedore sits moodily on the edge of his filthy bed, slowly scratching his bare back, then picking the lice from beneath his nails. Each time he has killed one of them between his two thumb-nails, he crosses his arms over his hairy chest and rocks backwards and forwards, as if in pain or prayer, before resuming his toilet. . .

". . . Surreptitiously, an old Armenian bawd draws back the curtain of her window and watches me as I approach her door. In her tottering wooden tenement, the stairs creak beneath the stealthy tread of the whispering girls who wait there, shivering in their soiled night-gowns, desperately hoping that I'll squander a fortune on their doubtful charms. Or am I the unusual stranger, the apparently harmless prelude to a massacre? Catastrophe always begins imperceptibly, on a small scale, disguised at first as innocuous accident. Hesitating as I walk up the deserted alley, I seem to be as fearful or as hopeful as they, testing the day gingerly like the water of a pool before diving into the unknown that is still the future. . .

". . . The wear and tear of a thousand years has left the city as fragmentary as any atom-bomb's crater. . ."

JOURNAL OF A TRIP

I.

The Long Walk

—"How many more miles?"
—"To . . . ?"
—"How far have we already come?"
—"From . . . ?"
—"Are we going in the right direction?"
—"How should I know? We never had a map or a compass, and clouds conceal the moon and stars. . ."
I can no longer remember when nor whence we set forth. Because we know that we can never find our way back to our starting-point, and since there is never any good reason for us to stop and settle in any place rather than anywhere else, we go doggedly ahead. How could we find our way back through lands of which we remember only the weather that concealed from our enquiring eyes every possible landmark? Everywhere the weather has been equally inclement, though differing according to seasons which seem to follow an unpredictable order. When we crossed mountain-ranges, it was drizzling and we could never see even the tree-tops; because we trod on thick composts of rotting leaves, we believed that it was autumn and that the trees—we could distinguish only their trunks in the mist—were leafless. Now it is probably winter, though autumn that I have just described was followed by a season which might well have been spring, after which it was colder, till the ravines are now full of snow, as far as we can see through the mist that is also as white as snow. But some streams that we cross are dry, as if in summer, while others are swollen with raging waters and others again are flowing, if at all, beneath a thick layer of ice. At one time too, it must have been summer; the air was warm, but so moist that we seemed to be living in a cloud of steam.
On our way, we meet others, all wandering as blindly as we in these shrouded landscapes. When we speak to them, none of them can make much sense of our speech, nor can we ever understand theirs. Were we now to turn back, would we ever meet any of them again? Sometimes, in the snow, we stumble on the corpse of a wanderer who, as lost as we are too, appears to

have died on his way. The men and women that we once met as we went are now dead or have wandered elsewhere. Would we even know it, were we ever to meet one of them again? They were all alike, almost reflections of ourselves, as featureless as we too have become. A couple of days ago, I chanced to catch a glimpse of my own face reflected in a mirror, like a faded photograph that I could barely recognize.

Sometimes, we discover the ruins of an abandoned city. On a table in a deserted tavern, near a tumbler of wine that had evaporated and left a dark stain in the dusty glass, I once found a book, printed in an unknown alphabet and illustrated with maps of what appeared to be imaginary continents. In the ruins of a building that had probably been a church or a temple, I was able to recognize the altar: it stood beneath the disfigured images of an utterly alien god.

Somewhere, we met an old woman, garrulously eager to converse with us. Though we failed to understand what she muttered, she insisted on offering us an herb that we obtained from her in exchange for a few coins of an unknown currency that still happened to rattle in my otherwise empty pocket and that seemed to puzzle her as much as they also puzzled me. With gestures, she gave us to understand that we should chew this herb that we purchased from her. Though we already remembered very little of our previous travels, its juices soon helped us to forget what few memories still haunted our minds, like moth-eaten clothes forgotten in an abandoned closet. But we also found this herb refreshing when we were reduced to chewing it to slake our thirst as we crossed a desert.

We travel light. Why carry cumbersome loot from lands that we forget so easily? Why cherish the memory of people, places and things that each man remembers differently, if at all, so that no two memories of a single thing can ever tally? We no longer seem to be afflicted with any real needs; though we might once have felt that our present condition is one of extreme poverty, we regret no lost riches, scarcely ever remembering what we may once have been proud to own and display.

Still, we have known moments when everything was more clear than now, when we could see where we were and remember whence we came. There have been nights, for instance, when the clouds suddenly dispersed so as to reveal to our searching eyes an expanse of clear sky, spangled with bright stars. But their constellations always appear to be entirely new, unlike any of our remembered notions of celestial order. Nowhere can we then distinguish a single star that might be one which we know by name and which can guide us. Instead of one Evening Star, we were thus able, one night, to distinguish two, each one of them shining brightly in an unwonted area of the sky.

I remember too how we once reached, after crossing a desert in a blinding sand-storm, an abandoned city that tallied exactly with my memories of another city, except that the latter, unless I am mistaken, had stood in the midst of a well-watered, fertile and populous plain. I could still find my way very easily through the familiar maze of this city's deserted streets, as if I had lived there all my life. One of my companions—or was it my own divided mind correcting me?—insisted however that this same city reminded him, because of its battlements and towers, of one that he had once seen in hilly country, far from any desert or any fertile plain.

Nobody is known to have ever returned from the land that we believe to be our ultimate destination. When we cross deserts, whatever tracks we still find in the sands, if the winds have not yet smoothed them out, lead us ahead like sign-posts, never back towards the past. We thus know that many have gone ahead of us. Though we sometimes overtake others who, exhausted, travel more slowly, we have never yet met a single man or woman who was going in the opposite direction, back to our lost and almost forgotten country of origin.

Every one of our days has clearly been the yesterday of others who lived wherever we happen to be, but long before we came. Each city that we discover on our way is surrounded by a vast necropolis, an area of cemeteries far larger than that city itself. In some of these cities, we have met a few recluses who remained there when the bulk of the population drifted away, leaving them to live among abandoned ruins. But they are dull-witted natives, incapable of any intelligible speech and generally quite senile, except for a few wanderers like ourselves, stragglers who have stopped there to rest for a few days. Nobody can ever tell us the history of such a city, explaining to us when it was built, who lived there and why it was later abandoned. From the objects that we find in the deserted houses, we can only presume that the city's economy and culture remained for a long while at their peak before beginning to deteriorate. Everything that we find is old and worn, as if there had long been an acute shortage of able-bodied craftsmen to supply anything new. But we also find unspoiled foods awaiting us everywhere, though never more than we might need. Had our arrival been announced and expected? Who takes care of our needs, never lavishing on us more than might be strictly necessary? What instinct drives us unerringly to those few houses where we can satisfy our modest needs, rather than to the many other houses which are no more dilapidated but which we enter later, out of sheer curiosity, only to discover that we were fortunate not to have penetrated them earlier, when we were still hungry?

Crumbling beneath the weight of their past that crushes them, these cities are doomed to disappear very soon, dissolving into the landscape from which they once crystallized. Like obsolete figures of speech that have become meaningless, they can only puzzle us, failing to communicate to us their history. Because they offer us no information, we soon forget them, though some detail of their architecture may yet haunt our minds for a long while, like something remembered from a dream, both disturbingly familiar and frighteningly alien.

—"How many are still in our party?"

—"Each time I count our straggling group, I reach a different sum, fewer or more than when I last counted."

—"Have you tried a roll-call?"

—"No, I don't know their names, not even yours."

—"Ask them to call out their names and draw up a list of them."

—"I'll begin with you. . . "

—"But I've forgotten my own name since we chewed that herb."

—"Haven't we all chewed that herb, to quench our thirst when we were crossing the desert? From no longer being loved, are we not all equally nameless? We all look alike, yet we change as new ones join our group while others drop out. When we reach our goal, perhaps each one of us will suddenly remember who he is, when he came, and can register. . ."

—"Some reach our destination sooner than others. Some, I've been told, reach it before they have had time to learn to speak or to read and write, some even before they have been given a name."

—"But somebody must keep a count of us, even of those who are nameless."

—"Why try to count what cannot be counted?"

—"Are we so numerous?"

—"As numerous as the sands of the storm that blinded us in the desert, though we may sometimes seem to be few because we can discern only those who happen to be close to us."

—"Who would ever believe that death has undone so many men or that those of us who at any time are alive are so pitifully few?"

II.

The Goal

After we had successfully stamped out the present, we were ready to love and let love. But our feet, as we danced, were at first still sore, blistered from treading on the burning coals of war and strife, now reduced to cold and lifeless ashes. Should we at least proclaim the end of the Reign of Error, legalize drugs and homosexuality because no longer at all necessary, burn all our money together with yesterday's newspapers that have become meaningless and useless, celebrate inflation as a Holy Sacrament in an eternally rising market, stop the War on Poverty and rejoice in our freedom from affluence, be content with minimal art in an age of universal inspiration?

For reality's poisons, we no longer need any antidotes. Light as air, luminously beautiful, we are wingless angels, purged of original sin and able to subsist on mere perfumes as sweet to our sense of smell as the prayers of saints in the nostrils of our late Maker, recently deceased. From the waist downwards, we are pure spirit, no longer the slaves of sex nor ever obliged to excrete. None of us is now tempted, like a mad spider, to unravel yesterday's web and travel, following the thread of his memories through the labyrinth of his past, back to the womb; nor is anyone interested, like a prophetic surveyor, in measuring with the theodolite of foresight the distance that still separates him from his tomb.

Though our precarious eternity may be doomed to expire at any moment, though we have no lease on breath, who cares? We are squatters in the limitless meadows of timelessness and enjoy it, knowing that nothing, even our joy, can ever be truly real.

III.

Questions & Answers

Keep it cool. Take it easy. Keep what? Take what? Yourself, your own reality. Drop out. Out of where? Out of your mind, out of this world. Turn off. Off what? Yourself, everything. Tune in. On what? Yourself, nothing.

When and where? If not now, then never. If not here, then nowhere. Add up the sum of everything, divide all by you, here and now, with an end of beginnings.

IV.

Variations on a Whimper

This way out!

With a hysterical keening, with weeping and gnashing of teeth, for the very wealthy who have paid for it all in advance;

Without a word or a sign, in a vast peaceful landscape where the ploughman turns his back on the distant sea and the great ship sails majestically away, for the diminutive hero who fell from the heavens into the calm bay;

With a brief paid announcement in the local press, for most people whom we happen to know or not know;

With emphatic headlines and much verbiage, with organ-music broadcast from all stations and then two minutes of silence when the traffic stops dead and the tickers refrain from transmitting news and market-quotations, for those whom we should be glad to have lost, for the principalities and powers, for the presidents and policy-makers;

With a crackling of burning tinder, a great deal of acrid smoke and finally a pile of ashes and rubble, for the masterpieces of the art of all nations and the hundred great books;

With a rustling of paper, the rattling of a chain and a brief rush of water, for the memory of a contemporary poet, yours truly.

Inventions
(1938-1970)

THE FALL OF MAN

for Nicolas Calas

A man of water, moving statue,
With rainbow veins and eyes, awakes
From our dark dream, steps into day
While we, asleep, invent our night.

The garden knows his godlike touch
And flowers fawn for dew beneath
His jewelled hands. What gardener
Can bless caressingly as he?

He leaves no tracks but dew across
The paths and lawns which he revives;
His tread's too gentle to disturb
The worm's nocturnal tunnelings.

The sun is proud to shine for him,
Who glistens in each glistening beam;
And birds festoon the trees with song
To greet the silent listener.

The whole world, delicately spaced,
Hangs from a hawk that, hovering high,
Catches the sunlight on its wings
And pins our hopes of peace to heaven.

That bird, betrayed by greed, now swoops
To kill what mouse? A sudden cloud
Conceals the sun. Our visitor,
The fountain man, must fall and faint

To a muddy puddle. A shrill clock screams.
Mothered in the caverns of his sleep,
The widowed gardener first farts,
Kicks his bedfellow, curses loud

And, pasty-eyed, turns to rape
His son, pleasure before day's toil.

Then, breakfasting on garlicked bread,
And hurriedly dressed sallies forth

To piss into the puddled god.

POEM ABOUT NOTHING

The dream-world of the kangaroo
Is known to none: "For here be men
With heads of fish, transparent birds
And beasts of leaves, and singing plants. . ."

His antipodic fantasies,
Realms of pure speculation,
Are virgin soil, but with no future,
No West where caravans will crowd.

A desert mind, intact, unchanging
As the myriad days or years go by
Leaving no ruins, no Valley of Kings,
And promising no Golden Age,

It's autotelic as a poem,
Neither bought, nor sold, nor hoarded,
But there in pure being, itself its end
And beginning, without rhyme or reason.

THE CUSTOMER IS ALWAYS RIGHT

The lady who is never wrong
Is our best customer.
Piecemeal she purchases the town,
But she is hard to please.

We think up twenty things a day
To lure her gaze away from us:
She'll take them all, and take us too,
Though none knows when she'll choose nor why.

Neglected, all of us speak ill
Of her whose favor we most fear.
She's faithful too: there's no escape
For all the millions that she loves.

No mirror will reflect her face,
But she will buy and break them all.
She's deaf, yet every violin
Serenades her in its dying fall.

Derived from junk-yards of the past,
Her income swells from year to year;
On future too she holds a lien,
Foreclosing as the days go by.

And all that is, will be or was
Is hers and hers alone,
Lock, stock and barrel, flotsam and jetsam
Cast upon her beach or drifting by.

FOUR ALLEGORIES OF LOVE

I.

Oedipus Is the Sphynx

Piercing the prison-walls of years
Piled up more stiff than stone, more strict,
My loud-mouthed orator, Memory,

Dissolves them with his flickering tongue,
Stammers again, Demosthenes
Rolling his ruined prison yet

As he wanders along the broad seashore
And harangues the waves and mouths
Broken years, broken stones, broken words.

The beach, beyond horizon's scope,
Circles the world, I know, measured,
By other groups, figures on a clock.

Here two men fight, one tall, one small.
What giant-killer this who wants
To kill his Titan self and seeks

To tear with huge and hairy hands
His own tongue, the Other's, from its roots
And feels no pain or loves his pain?

I'll swear my riddle might remain
Unanswered, puzzling even me
Who dreamed the dream and write it now;

But Love's the answer, love and speech,
Both feared too long for fear of pain
Till my frustration brought me pain.

The Language of Flowers

She's none too clever. Born and bred
A lady, she yet twists and grinds
My tender orchid in too-eager hands

To minced meat. Where's my beautiful,
My bloom, my bounty mutinied
Too soon, then mutilated too?

She's dumb; but so am I. Just teach
Her some reason, or teach me, and each
Knows when to stop and when begin.

Her rose might then dwell by my flower
And smell as sweet, sharing my name
If need be, and my bloom stay fresh.

III.

Caliban

The lady with the lemon-drops
Strung round her neck, and sugared feet,
Trod on my heart. How bitter-sweet
Her dominion, my lowly estate!

Her man, an ugly bird at that,
Disdains me too, with suede-shod toes
Spurning my God-made body. Who knows?
I may revolt, then I may not.

Is there an end? Remember
The first kick. Or was there ever one,
Or a night before the moon or a day before the sun?
I've lived in mud a million years,

True to my slime-mould ancestry
That slowly, jealous of the stars,
Grew nucleus and spine, then scales or furs,
Then hairless limbs, and still reached up,

But failed and fell. My starless hands
Are full of mud, but oh, too late,
For the biter cannot now be bait
And the fallen god is not a goon.

IV.

The Gladiator on the Chessboard

Asbestos queens who feel no pain
And know not what my labors cost
Spitefully cheer each time I fail;

And I'm both slave and lion within
The circus of their lordly gaze
Who gave me birth and want my death.

Yet I must fight against myself
And all the world to prove my worth
If only by my vast mistakes.

For theirs the Kingdom, Dames of Hell
Who gave me body and soul at odds
Each with the other and with them;

And theirs the Power, who taught me all
I know or ever ought to know,
These goddesses ungodly too.

This is the set-up: a game with rules
Within which I must toil and cheat,
Transgressing only when there's doubt;

And mine the Glory, should I ever
Know more than I'm supposed to know
And outwit them and mate their king.

MANHATTAN NOVELETTES

I.

The Lorelei with the spaghetti hair
Queens it at the raw-meat piano
While her heliotropic audience pays
A thousand looks for every note.

Desperate beneath her platformed feet,
Her rubber lover sweats pure oil;
He's jealous of his snoring neighbor,
The Hairy Ainu with a dyed mink face.

Both men now think her heels are round,
Since each in turn has been her beau
Though neither long enough to know
That art's her love and love her art.

II.

Nursing his beer until it boils,
The boy whose fall cost but a dime
Watches the blonde with parrot voice
And hopes she'll whisper love at last.

This pretty polly knows her stuff.
She's no sad sister: hard as nails,
She'll trail her man through fog or fen
And turn her dollar, come what may.

And come who may, by hook or crook,
He'll think this houri's worth her price;
He'll never find, concealed beneath
The feathers smooth, bird-claw, bird-beak.

134

III.

The subway cowboy with a midnight tan
Texas of sex will nightly roam;
He'll sell his body to any devil
For a greenback dollar bill.

For a greenback dollar bill or two
He'd sell his soul. But who will pay
Visible coin for invisible wares,
Temporal for eternal, who?

All for a greenback dollar bill,
What Wests can we discover yet
Who roam Manhattan's midnight range
From neonrise to neonset?

New York, 1942

THE IDENTITY OF CONTRARIES

I dream I'm mad, and in my madness
Am far more sane than in a dream
Or when awake, for fear of being
Found mad by dream-companions.

My sanity's daily madness,
To a watchful world attributing
More watchfulness and deep concern
For my reason than reason warrants.

My daily life's a dream, each day
Concealing, simulating till
Reason and madness are alike
And when I dream I'm acting.

In dream, my sanity and madness,
In madness, dream and daily life,
All mingle, each aping the other:
Dreaming or awake, I'm mad and sane.

THE NATURE OF KNOWLEDGE

for Alexander Koval

I.

From the marketless star whose staple is poetry,
In the huge perspective of deadly wisdom,
Behold how lines meet only in illusion.

Only there, in the endless end, can you watch
The incredible dream changing, changing,
Equal to itself, in change most changeless.

Knowledge, with its almanacs and catalogues
Outdated daily, knows no end
And no beginning. Be but wise,

Not knowing; discerning, not good; or else
Join the killers and the killed who wrangle,
Come peace or war, in courage and conviction.

II.

In the veering hesitancy of a breeze
That's free to blow, but knows no aim,
See this world's slavery, constrained

By aimlessness, an ignorance.
On the empty shore, the gull and the clown
Swap wisdom in long dialogues

Where neither understands the other.
But fate, patron saint of all fools,
Dovetails each answer to fit its question;

And none's the wiser, nor more foolish,
Though this feathered Socrates and spangled Kant
Agree or disagree with the ebb and flow

Of culture, another moon-ruled tide.
Thus knowledge, wise as a wave or a woman,
Follows its course from nowhere to nowhere.

III.

In love's swift foretaste of death
When the unblinking eye sees the Beast in Beauty
There's sudden knowledge, soon forgotten
As the heart returns to its stubborn task.

Wonderful as water in a glass
And as common, sleep each night
Slakes our thirst for what we once knew
That unremembered now teases our memory.

In the anagram of a dream concealed
The great fear lurks, to be deciphered
If you know the key, else you must wait
For the dreamless night that leads to no dawn.

Then all knowledge, vouchsafed at last,
Is useless as ignorance, and who cares?
In death's same boat, the wise and the fool
Drift forever, each unaware of the other.

COLD WAR BULLETINS

for Alain Bosquet

1. Historic meeting

The airlifting of forbidden fruit
Into blockaded hells
Began when the military governors
Returned, from a convivial fork-lunch

Where they had eaten their caps and their heads,
To an interrupted Council meeting;
But they now had no lips to utter
The Four-power words that might shake the world.

For obvious security reasons
This wonder was hushed up:
The press had likewise neglected
To report our President's pregnancy.

Nature's pranks no longer puzzle
Human kind whose science, an angry bomb,
May destroy the known world at any moment.
But censorship, our conscience, still prevails.

2. Panic in the powder-room

And were it to happen now,
What you most fear, a split girdle
Or an atom-bomb, are you ready,
All made up to meet your Maker?

3. Tit for Tat

With the neatness of retribution
In a dramatist's dream of life,
We're pursued by unrelenting fears
Of the secret weapons of our enemies

139

Whom we plan, as we tinker our gadgets,
To destroy—how or when, who knows?—
With a bang that may burst our world
But must surely release us from fear.

4. On a former Trotskyst turned Cold-war propagandist

He never earned as much until
He turned his coat. Instead of sil-
ver linings, as in songs, a green-
back salary could then be seen.

5. I'm a stranger here myself

The land of milk and honey
Where never a poker-game is lost
And love is plentiful as money
And no flower need fear frost:

That's my home state. But here,
I'm an exile, arbitrarily driven
Out of my past that was Heaven
Into this Hell of a year.

Berlin, 1947

NORTH BEACH, SAN FRANCISCO

for George Hitchcock

I.

A tragic muse, now unemployed
In an age that eschews verse drama,
Tried her luck as a topless waitress
In a Titburger Heaven for the weekend trade.

Serving champagne breakfasts after Sunday Mass
She kept her customers in tears
Of pity and contrition. Weary of laughter,
A comic muse retired from the stage

And took her vows in a Carmelite convent.
Her silences made the nuns shriek with joy.
There's a time and place for every face
And never a fish that drowns.

II.

The topless weddings of the damned
Are celebrated aboard
A ship of fools that forever sails
The waters of the Bottomless Pit.

The captain is their curate and recites
The Mass backwards, untying the knot
That once bound them in matrimony
Till he leaves them free from adultery.

After the ceremony, they crowd on the deck
To cast their gold rings on the waves
And watch the fish leap to swallow them.
In a pickled mackerel I once found a ring.

San Francisco, 1970

141

CATOPTOMANTIC POEM

for Lawrence and Justine Fixel

Catapulted across the causeway
By a wild dog in hot pursuit,
Katinka Cat barely escaped
Catastrophe beneath the wheel

Of a passing car. Later that day
Fate's concatenations allowed
Her to recover her natural poise
By reducing a mouse to mere catsup.

Our proverbial catechism teaches
That one cat's meat is another's poison,
But no catharsis through pity or fear
Can mend Katinka's cattish ways.

A catalogue of any cat's actions
From cat's cradle to cat's grave,
Devoid of ethics, no decalogue,
Will always deny all but instinct's

Categorical imperatives.

THE EGOCENTRIC

A pregnant computer, pondering
The wages of sin, input, output
And feedback too, felt that its fate

Was worse than death. Any other
Unmarried mother deserved less pity.
Misfortune is mine, never yours.

OBITUARY FOR A BEDBUG

On the humblest of my plagues I vent
My full destructive rage. It dies
As soon as I've detected it.

Were my insecticidal range
As broad as I might wish, I'd live
The life of Riley, free from taxes,

Wars in Vietnam, door-to-door salesmen
And any other plague or pest
That irks me more than a mere itch.

HOUSEHOLD HINTS: A BESTIARY

for Dan Halpern

The preposterous hippopotamus
Is boisterously unprepossessing.
Try keeping some at home as pets:
Day in, day out, you'll be shovelling turds.

Keep carrion-fed vultures in a cage
Or a school of whales in a basement tank,
An elephant in a frontyard kennel,
Performing fleas in your guestroom bed.

Keep a mermaid as mistress or marry her:
If allergic to fish, you'll be covered with hives.
Think of all the disasters you've been spared
And bless reality for what it is.

THE SECRET SHIP

for Mario Cesariny de Vasconcelos

Between the waters and the sky
A ship of mirrors reflects
All that reflects it and itself.

Like tentacles, its roots reach out
To strangle fish. Its shimmering sails
And ropes of glass are snares for gulls.

The winds that swell its sheets, the waves
That toss its brittle timbers strain
To pluck such harplike harmonies

Out of its voyage that its hold
Must echo like an instrument
Beneath its deck that no feet tread.

It sailed from no known port and heads
For nowhere in its endless quest,
Unmanned, unseen, a secret ship.

Edouard Roditi

Printed September 1974 in Santa Barbara &
Ann Arbor for the Black Sparrow Press by
Noel Young & Edwards Brothers Inc.
Design by Barbara Martin. This edition
is published in paper wrappers; there are
200 hardcover copies numbered & signed by
the poet; & 50 numbered copies handbound
in boards by Earle Gray signed by the poet
& containing an original numbered etching
by Jose Hernandez.

200

PHOTO: GREGORY A. PEARSON

Born in Paris in 1910 of an American father, Edouard Roditi has always been an American citizen, but attended schools in France and England, then Oxford University, before coming to the United States for the first time in 1929. By then, he had already published poems and prose in English and in French in **transition** and a number of other American, English, French and expatriate periodicals. These publications included, in 1929, the first Surrealist Manifesto to be written and published in English.

Until 1937, he continued to live in Europe, then attended the University of Chicago and the University of California at Berkeley. From 1937 until 1946, he lived in the United States, after which he returned to Europe as an interpreter for the Nuremberg War Crimes Trials. Since 1946, he has continued to live in Europe, at first in Berlin and now in Paris. Although active in Europe as a free-lance multilingual simultaneous interpreter for Unesco, the European Common Market and other international agencies, he generally returns every year to the United States to teach or lecture during the winter months.

He has now published extensively in American, English, French and German periodicals, especially in the fields of literary criticism and art history, and has been a guest professor of English or French literature or of art history at the University of California, at Brown University and elsewhere. His published books include: **Oscar Wilde** (in the "Makers of Modern Literature" series, New Directions, 1947), **Poems 1928-1948** (New Directions, 1949), **Dialogues on Art** (Horizon Books, 1961), **Prose Poems: New Hieroglyphic Tales** (Kayak Press, San Francisco, 1968), and **Magellan of the Pacific** (McGraw-Hill, 1973), as well as a number of translations from French, German, Dutch and Turkish.